Editor's letter

David **Morris**
Author/Editor

AI Life is your new go-to guide to demystifying the tools and tricks that quietly shape modern life. We're not here to overwhelm you with technical jargon or predict robot uprisings. Instead, we show you exactly how Artificial Intelligence (AI) already works in your world—and how to make it work better for you.

Brought to you by AI experts with real-world experience, each issue maps the AI landscape from your kitchen to your workplace, and hands you practical activities to try today. We test the tools, decode the hype, and translate complex concepts into weekend projects you'll actually want to tackle.

Think less "science fiction", more "supercharged life hacks". Every article delivers something you can use immediately, whether you're a student cramming for exams, a professional drowning in emails, or a retiree exploring new hobbies.

DISCOVERING

- **First encounters**: AI is no longer futuristic—it's in your everyday life
- **Our connected world**: Your smart devices aren't just connected—they're learning from you every day
- **Deep dive**: Roll up your sleeves—get hands-on experience generating results in just minutes
- **Spotlight**: See how AI can benefit anyone—from students to seniors
- **Ask an AI expert**: Bust the myths and hype with our expert Q&A

Read cover to cover or dip in wherever you like.

HANDS-ON LEARNING

Every **Deep dive** article includes real projects you can complete in 15-30 minutes. For example, in **ChatGPT—your brainstorming buddy who never sleeps** (on page 46), you'll tackle your first challenge: planning a weekend city break. You'll see exactly how to refine prompts, customize responses, and turn generic suggestions into personalized plans. No guesswork—just clear steps and real results.

LET US KNOW

Have a question, tip, or AI hack that changed your routine? Email us at *AILife@ineasysteps.com*. We read every message and will feature the best reader discoveries in future issues.

GET STARTED

Let's make AI work for us, not the other way around. This isn't about replacing human creativity or judgment—it's about amplifying what you already do well and reclaiming time for what matters most.

Ready to get started? Turn to **What is AI and why should you care?** on page 7, or jump straight to any section that catches your eye. Your AI journey begins now. ■

David Morris

AI Life and **In easy steps** are imprints of
In Easy Steps Limited
16 Hamilton Terrace
Holly Walk
Leamington Spa
Warwickshire
CV32 4LY
United Kingdom

First edition – Issue one

Contents.

First encounters

Start here: get grounded in why AI isn't sci-fi but part of your every day

What is AI and why should you care?

Imagine your phone auto-tagging your vacation photos before you've even opened the gallery. While you're still waiting to board your return flight, it's already organized "beach day", "sunset dinner", and "kids playing" into neat collections. You didn't teach it these categories–it learned them from watching how you've tagged photos before.

Having spent the last 10 years working with teams across many enterprises—as well as embracing the emerging technology at home too—here's what I've learned about AI that every curious consumer should know.

Why AI matters to you today

AI isn't coming to transform your life someday—it's already saving you time, improving your experience, and making decisions on your behalf right now. Here are three ways it's likely working for you already:

Smarter photos: Your camera's AI turns those dim restaurant shots into share-worthy memories. It recognizes faces, adjusts lighting, and even suggests the best moment from a burst of photos—all automatically.

Time saved: Email apps now summarize long threads and suggest replies, trimming 15 minutes from your morning routine. Instead of reading through dozens of messages, you get the key points in seconds.

Health nudges: Your smartwatch doesn't just count steps—it learns your patterns and warns you when you've been sitting for too long, suggests breathing exercises when your heart rate spikes, and even detects irregular rhythms.

These aren't futuristic concepts. They're features you're probably using right now without realizing the sophisticated technology behind them.

What exactly is AI?

Boiling it down into plain language, AI—short for Artificial Intelligence—is software that learns patterns in data and then makes recommendations, decisions, or predictions. Think of it as pattern recognition on steroids—it spots connections and trends that would take humans hours, days, or sometimes years to identify.

When your music app creates a "Discover Weekly" playlist, it's analyzing your listening history, comparing it to millions of other users' habits, and predicting songs you'll like based on patterns in the data. When your email flags a message as spam, it's recognizing patterns it learned from analyzing billions of previous emails.

The three key components

Every AI system works through three essential steps:

Data ingestion—feeding the beast: AI needs examples to learn from. Your phone's camera AI has been trained on millions of photos to recognize faces, objects, and scenes. The more examples it sees, the better it gets at making accurate predictions.

Model training—finding hidden trends: AI analyzes all that data to identify patterns

Our connected world

See how AI quietly powers the home assistants, appliances, and systems you already use.

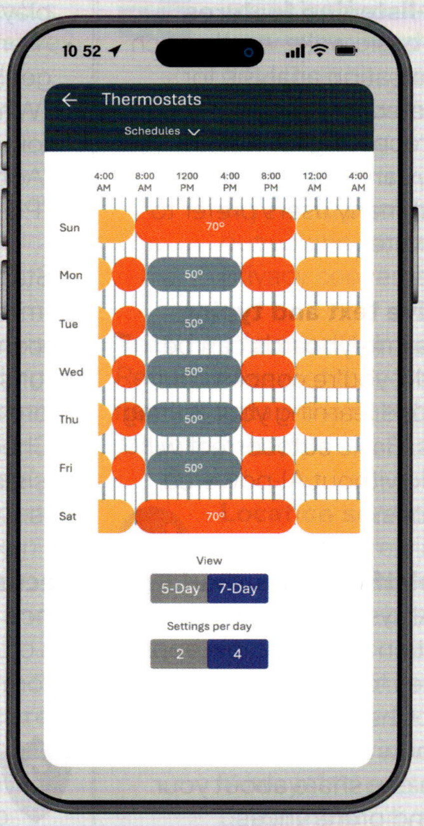

Smarter homes–embrace connected living

Your thermostat quietly drops the temperature two degrees at 10:47 PM. The coffee maker starts brewing at 6:15 AM, five minutes before your alarm. Lights gradually brighten in the hallway as you pad toward the kitchen. Your home just made several decisions without you lifting a finger.

This isn't science fiction—it's just a Tuesday morning in millions of homes. Smart home technology has moved beyond the novelty phase into genuine daily convenience. The average connected home saves families $180 annually on energy costs alone, while eliminating dozens of small daily tasks that add up to hours of saved time each week.

The brains behind the magic

Smart devices earn their name through embedded Artificial Intelligence (AI) that learns from your behavior and anticipates your needs. The difference between "connected" and truly "smart" lies in Machine Learning algorithms that observe, adapt, and predict.

Traditional programmable thermostats require you to set schedules manually. Smart thermostats like the Nest Learning Thermostat watch your behavior for a week, then start adjusting temperatures automatically. They notice you leave for work at 8:30 AM on weekdays but sleep in on Saturdays. They track which rooms you use most, and when you prefer cooler temperatures for sleeping.

How smart devices learn

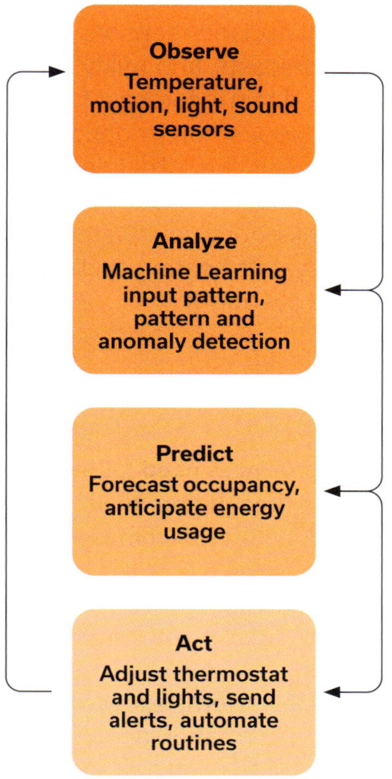

Pattern recognition in action

The AI behind these devices uses pattern recognition to build models of your daily life. Machine Learning algorithms process thousands of data points—when you arrive home, how quickly you adjust the temperature, which lights you turn on first, and how long you spend in different rooms. Over time, these systems become surprisingly accurate at predicting what you want before you realize you want it.

Modern smart homes integrate multiple data sources for better predictions. Your smart thermostat might connect with your phone's GPS to start cooling the house when you're five minutes away, or sync with your calendar to run the dishwasher during your two-hour meeting when noise won't matter.

The most sophisticated systems combine occupancy sensors, weather forecasts, and utility rate schedules. If rain is forecast for tomorrow, your smart irrigation system cancels the scheduled watering. If electricity rates spike during peak hours, your water heater delays its heating cycle until rates drop overnight.

Hot Tip

Most smart devices need 1-2 weeks of "learning time" before their automated features become truly helpful.

Data integration for smarter decisions

Smart home systems excel when they share information across devices. Your security system's motion sensors can tell your thermostat which rooms are actually occupied, while your smart doorbell can trigger pathway lights when it detects a delivery truck approaching. Weather data influences everything from irrigation schedules to when your smart blinds close automatically during intense afternoon sun.

Voice assistants serve as central command centers, processing requests and coordinating responses across multiple devices. Tell Alexa "I'm leaving for work", and your integrated system can lock doors, adjust temperatures, turn off unnecessary lights, and arm security cameras—all with a single command.

Climate control that thinks ahead

Smart thermostats serve as a gateway to home automation—and for good reason. They deliver immediate, measurable benefits while requiring minimal technical setup. Most models install in under an hour, and start saving money from day one.

The learning algorithms in devices like the Ecobee Smart Thermostat and Honeywell T9 go far beyond simple scheduling. They develop detailed profiles of your comfort preferences across different times, weather conditions, and seasons. The systems note that you prefer 72 degrees while working from home but tolerate 68 degrees when you're away for more than four hours.

Learning your preferences

Advanced models use "geofencing" technology that creates virtual boundaries around your home. When your smartphone crosses these invisible lines, your thermostat receives a signal to start adjusting temperatures. Leave for your morning commute, and the system automatically enters Away mode. Return from dinner, and the house starts cooling or warming before you reach the front door.

Room-by-room control represents the next evolution in smart climate systems. The Ecobee Smart Thermostat comes with wireless room sensors that detect both temperature and occupancy. If you're working in your home office all afternoon, the system prioritizes that room's comfort while letting unused bedrooms drift a few degrees warmer or cooler.

Seasonal learning patterns emerge over months of operation. Smart thermostats recognize that you prefer slightly warmer temperatures during winter months when daylight hours are shorter, or that your cooling preferences change during humid summer weather versus dry heat. These subtle adjustments happen automatically without any manual programming.

Did You Know?

Smart thermostats can detect when windows are open and temporarily suspend heating or cooling to avoid energy waste.

Energy savings that add up

Energy optimization happens automatically through Machine Learning. Smart thermostats analyze your usage patterns, local weather data, and your home's thermal characteristics to minimize energy waste. They learn how long your house takes to cool down on hot afternoons or warm up on cold mornings, then time their operations for maximum efficiency.

The financial benefits add up quickly. Energy Star estimates that smart thermostats save homeowners $180 per year on heating and cooling costs. In regions with extreme climates, savings often exceed $300 annually. Most smart thermostats pay for themselves within two to three years through energy savings alone.

Utility companies often offer rebates for smart thermostat installations, with discounts ranging from $50 to $200. Many power companies also offer time-of-use rates that smart thermostats can exploit automatically, running heating and cooling systems during off-peak hours when electricity costs less. Pacific Gas & Electric customers, for example, can save an additional $100 annually by shifting energy use to off-peak periods.

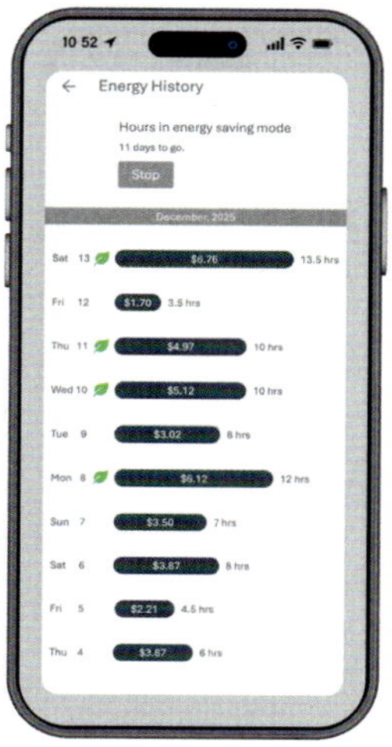

Quick Start

Setting up your first "automation schedule" takes less than 10 minutes using smartphone apps—start with basic away/home schedules.

1. Download your thermostat's smartphone app and create an account
2. Connect the thermostat to your home Wi-Fi network
3. Set your basic schedule for weekdays and weekends
4. Enable location-based automation using your phone's GPS
5. Let the system observe your behavior for 1-2 weeks before expecting optimal performance

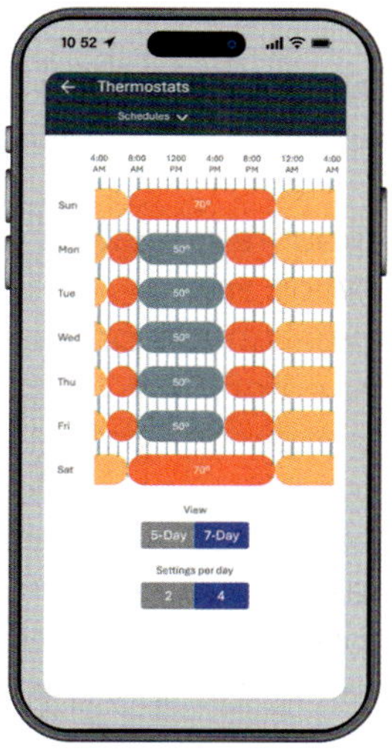

Lighting that follows your life

Smart lighting systems go far beyond dimming switches and colorful accent lights. Modern LED smart bulbs and switches create lighting environments that adapt to your daily rhythms, enhance your health, and improve your home's security.

Your body runs on a natural 24-hour clock called your "circadian rhythm"—the internal system that makes you feel alert during the day and sleepy at night. Smart lighting that follows these natural rhythms represents the most sophisticated application of AI in home lighting.

Health-focused automation

The science behind circadian lighting comes from research showing how different light wavelengths affect melatonin production and sleep quality. Smart lighting systems use your location data to sync with local sunrise and sunset times, creating personalized lighting schedules that support your body's natural clock. Studies show that proper circadian lighting can improve sleep quality by up to 42%, and increase daytime alertness by 25%.

Systems like Philips Hue automatically adjust color temperature throughout the day, providing bright, blue-rich light in the morning to promote alertness, then shifting to warm, amber tones in the evening to support natural sleep patterns.

Motion detection and occupancy sensing eliminate the need to fumble for light switches. Smart switches like those from Lutron Caseta detect movement and ambient light levels, turning lights on only when needed and dimming them based on available natural light. The AI learns your movement patterns—brightening hallway lights when you typically wake up for midnight bathroom trips, or keeping kitchen lights dim during your late-evening snack runs.

Presence sensors create truly hands-free lighting that follows you through your home. As you enter a room, lights gradually brighten to your preferred level. Leave the space, and they automatically dim or turn off after a brief delay to ensure you've actually left. The effect feels like having an invisible assistant who anticipates your lighting needs.

Warning

Smart lights can significantly increase your home's standby power consumption—in the US, look for Energy Star certified models. Other countries have similar standards—e.g. in the UK, it's EL (Energy Label).

Scenes and smart integration

"Scene" programming allows you to create custom lighting moods for different activities. "Movie Night" might dim all lights to 10% except for gentle accent lighting behind the TV. "Dinner Party" could set warm, flattering light throughout the main floor while keeping task lighting bright in the kitchen. "Reading Time" provides focused task lighting while dimming background illumination to reduce eye strain.

Advanced systems integrate with other smart home devices for comprehensive automation. When your smart lock detects you arriving home after dark, pathway lights illuminate automatically. When your security system arms for the night, all interior lights turn off except for a few safety lights in

Our connected world

hallways and stairwells. Morning routines can gradually brighten bedroom lights to simulate sunrise, making wake-up more natural and pleasant.

The most impressive smart lighting setups sync with natural light throughout the day. Lutron's natural light matching technology uses outdoor sensors to detect cloud cover and seasonal changes, adjusting indoor lighting to maintain consistent brightness levels regardless of weather conditions. This creates a seamless indoor-outdoor lighting experience that reduces eye strain and maintains productivity.

Energy savings come from precise control and LED efficiency. Smart lighting systems eliminate wasteful habits like leaving lights on in empty rooms, while LED bulbs use 75% less energy than traditional incandescent bulbs. The combination typically reduces lighting energy costs by 60-80% compared with conventional lighting. A typical home switching to smart LED lighting saves $75-$125 annually on electricity bills.

Quick Start

Creating Your First Lighting Scene.

1. Open your smart lighting app and select "Create Scene"
2. Choose which lights to include, and set their brightness levels
3. Adjust color temperature for the activity (warm for relaxation, cool for focus)
4. Test the scene and make adjustments
5. Set voice commands or automation triggers for easy activation

Kitchen intelligence

Smart kitchen appliances transform cooking from a series of manual tasks into a collaborative process with AI-powered assistants. These devices learn your cooking patterns, suggest meal improvements, and handle routine tasks automatically.

The Samsung Family Hub refrigerator exemplifies kitchen AI at work. Internal cameras photograph your food inventory each time you close the door, while AI algorithms identify items and track expiration dates. The system sends smartphone notifications when you're running low on essentials, and can even add items to your grocery shopping list automatically.

Smart food management

Advanced refrigerator AI goes beyond simple inventory tracking. The systems learn your consumption patterns, noting that you typically use milk faster during

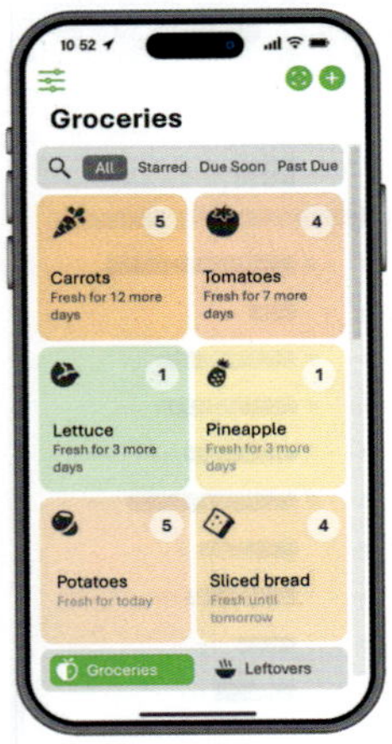

weeks when the kids are home from school, or that you buy fresh herbs but often forget to use them before they spoil. Based on these patterns, the AI adjusts shopping recommendations and sends timely reminders to use perishable items.

Inventory tracking extends beyond refrigerators to pantry management. Smart scales and container sensors monitor staple ingredients like flour, sugar, and coffee, automatically adding items to shopping lists when supplies run low. Some systems integrate with grocery delivery services like Amazon Fresh or Instacart, placing orders automatically based on your consumption patterns and preferred brands.

Quick Start

Setting Up Smart Food Tracking.

1. Install your refrigerator's companion app
2. Take initial photos of current food inventory
3. Enable expiration date notifications in app settings
4. Connect to your preferred grocery delivery service
5. Set up automatic reorder preferences for essentials like milk and eggs

Smart meal planning represents the next evolution in kitchen AI. Apps like Whisk connect with your smart appliances to suggest recipes based on available ingredients, dietary preferences, and cooking skill level. The systems learn which recipes you prepare successfully, and suggest variations based on seasonal ingredients or special dietary needs.

Next Level

Smart kitchen scales can automatically adjust recipe quantities and update shopping lists when you decide to double a recipe.

Cooking and cleaning automation

Smart ovens like the LG ThinQ series use AI to optimize cooking performance. The systems recognize different food types through internal cameras and sensors, then adjust cooking times and temperatures automatically. Load a frozen pizza, and the oven detects the size and thickness, then calculates the optimal cooking cycle for even heating and proper browning. More advanced models can even adjust cooking methods mid-cycle based on how food is browning or rising.

Coffee makers with AI scheduling learn your daily routines and prepare fresh coffee automatically. The Behmor Connected Coffee Maker monitors your morning schedule through smartphone integration, starting brewing cycles so that coffee finishes exactly when you typically enter the kitchen. The system adjusts for weekends, holidays, and travel schedules without manual reprogramming.

Whirlpool's load-sensing washing machines represent another kitchen AI success story. These systems weigh each load, analyze fabric types through water absorption patterns, and adjust water levels, agitation intensity, and cycle times accordingly. The AI learns your laundry habits—recognizing heavily soiled work clothes versus lightly worn casual items—and adapts washing cycles for optimal cleaning with minimal energy use.

Smart dishwashers from brands like Bosch use soil sensors to detect how dirty dishes are, then adjust water temperature, pressure, and cycle length automatically. The systems learn your loading patterns and dish types, optimizing spray patterns for your specific dishes and glassware. Energy savings average 15-25% compared with traditional dishwashers through precise water and energy usage.

Warning

Smart appliances collect usage data—check privacy settings to control what information gets shared.

Cleaning on autopilot

Robot vacuums have evolved from novelty gadgets into sophisticated cleaning systems that map your home, learn your preferences, and adapt to your lifestyle. Modern models like the iRobot Roomba and the Roborock series use AI to navigate efficiently while avoiding obstacles.

Smart mapping with lasers and cameras creates detailed floor plans of your home using precise measurements. The AI uses LiDAR (Light Detection and Ranging) to identify furniture, carpets, and room boundaries, then develops optimal cleaning patterns that maximize coverage while minimizing cleaning time. These systems remember multiple floor layouts—perfect for homes with multiple levels or frequent furniture rearrangement.

Smart navigation and learning

The learning algorithms observe your daily routines and adapt cleaning schedules accordingly. If you work from home on Tuesdays, the vacuum learns to clean your office after you typically leave for lunch. If you have pets that shed more during certain seasons, the system increases cleaning frequency automatically. Advanced models even recognize when you're hosting parties or gatherings, and suggest extra cleaning sessions.

Quick Start

First-Time Robot Vacuum Setup.

1. Clear floor areas of small objects and loose cables
2. Install charging station in accessible location with 3-feet clearance
3. Download the vacuum's app and connect to Wi-Fi
4. Run initial mapping cycle with all doors open
5. Set up virtual boundaries for areas you want to avoid
6. Schedule regular cleaning times that work with your routine

Obstacle recognition has become remarkably sophisticated. Modern robot vacuums identify and avoid pet toys, charging cables, and even pet waste—a feature that prevents the catastrophic "poop-ocalypse" scenarios that plagued earlier models. The AI learns the locations of furniture and decorative items, navigating

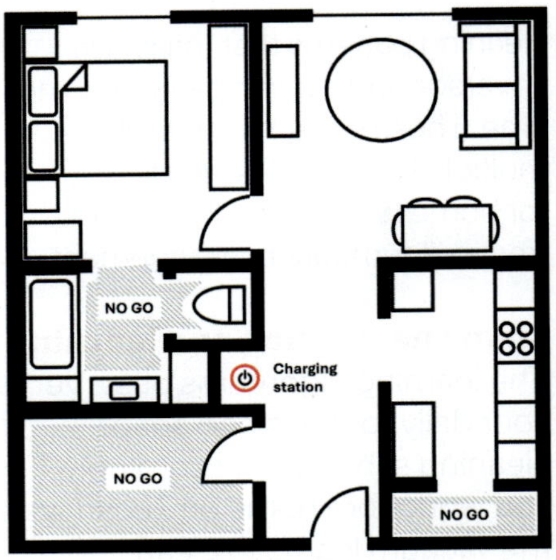

around them with increasing precision over time. Some models can detect different floor types and adjust suction power automatically for optimal cleaning on hardwood, tile, or carpet.

Pet behavior adaptation represents a major advancement in cleaning AI. Systems monitor pet activity patterns, noting where

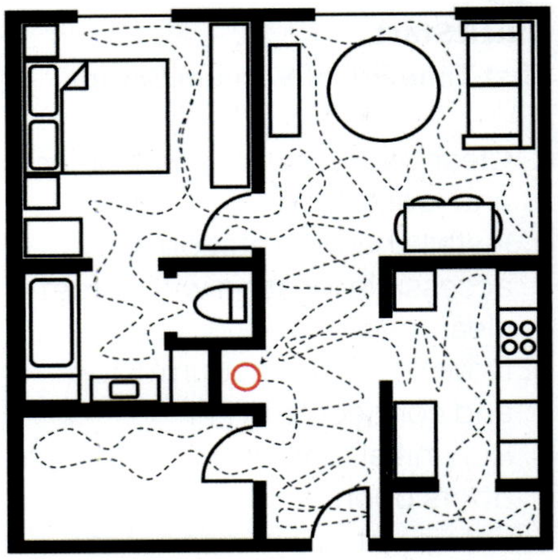

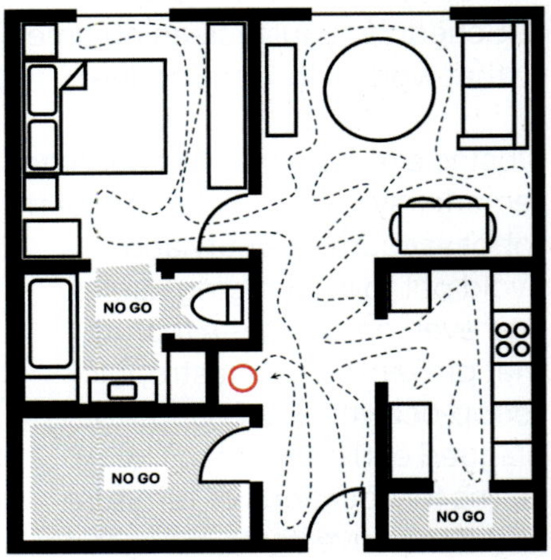

your dog likes to nap or where your cat tends to track litter. The vacuum adjusts its cleaning patterns to focus extra attention on these high-traffic areas while avoiding disrupting sleeping pets. During shedding seasons, the AI automatically increases cleaning frequency in areas where pets spend the most time.

Hot Tip

Robot vacuums work best when you "prep" your home by picking up small items, but they quickly learn which obstacles are permanent.

Targeted and automated cleaning

Zone cleaning allows you to target specific areas through smartphone apps. Spill something in the kitchen? Send the vacuum to clean just that room. Expecting guests? Focus extra cleaning attention on main living areas while skipping bedrooms. Some models offer "spot cleaning" that intensively cleans a small area multiple times for stubborn dirt or pet accidents.

Integration with other smart home devices creates comprehensive automation. Motion sensors can trigger spot cleaning when they detect unusually high activity in specific rooms. Smart doorbells can start cleaning cycles when they detect you leaving for work. Voice assistants allow hands-free control—simply say "Alexa, vacuum the living room", and the job gets done.

Multi-room cleaning becomes effortless with AI navigation. Advanced models return to their charging stations automatically when batteries run low, then resume cleaning exactly where they left off. The systems optimize

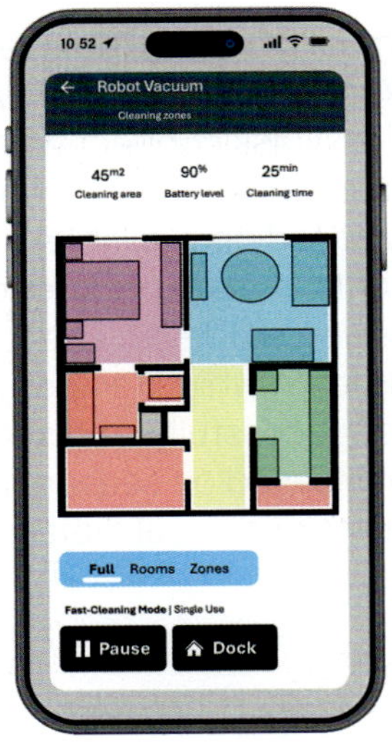

cleaning routes to minimize energy consumption while ensuring complete coverage. Battery management algorithms learn your home's size, and adjust cleaning intensity to complete full-home cleaning on a single charge.

Maintenance alerts keep your vacuum running efficiently. Smart models monitor brush wear, filter cleanliness, and dustbin capacity, sending smartphone notifications when maintenance is needed. Some premium models even order replacement parts automatically when sensors detect worn components.

Security and monitoring

Smart home security systems use AI to distinguish between legitimate threats and false alarms while providing comprehensive monitoring of your property. Modern security devices learn your family's patterns and adapt their responses accordingly.

Ring security cameras and doorbells integrate AI-powered person detection with smart home automation. The systems distinguish between people, vehicles, and animals, sending targeted alerts and triggering appropriate responses. A delivery truck might turn on pathway lights and send a notification, while a raccoon in the garden gets ignored. Advanced models can even recognize familiar faces and send personalized alerts like "John arrived home" versus generic "Person detected".

Quick Start

Smart Doorbell Installation Basics.

1. Turn off power at the circuit breaker for safety
2. Remove existing doorbell and note wire connections
3. Install mounting bracket using provided screws
4. Connect wires to new smart doorbell terminals
5. Restore power and test basic doorbell function
6. Download app and complete Wi-Fi setup

Intelligent threat detection

Facial recognition technology in smart doorbells and cameras learns to identify family members, regular visitors, and delivery personnel. The AI reduces false alarms by recognizing that your teenage daughter arriving home at 11 PM isn't a security threat, while still alerting you to unfamiliar faces during unusual hours. Privacy-conscious systems process facial recognition locally on the device rather than sending images to cloud servers.

Motion detection algorithms have become sophisticated enough to differentiate between wind-blown branches, passing cars, and actual security concerns. Smart cameras use AI to analyze movement patterns, size, and behavior to determine whether alerts are necessary. This reduces notification fatigue while ensuring genuine security events get immediate attention.

Integration with emergency services represents the cutting edge of smart security. Some systems can automatically contact local police or fire departments when they detect specific threats like broken glass, smoke, or unauthorized entry attempts. However, these features require careful configuration to prevent false emergency calls.

Warning

Smart security cameras that connect to the internet can be vulnerable to hacking—always change default passwords and enable two-factor authentication.

Access control and automation

Smart locks with AI capabilities learn your family's schedules and can automatically lock or unlock doors based on proximity detection and time patterns. Yale and August smart locks integrate with smartphones to unlock doors when family members approach, while staying securely locked for unfamiliar devices. The systems can provide temporary access codes for house cleaners, dog walkers, or guests, which automatically expire after specified time periods.

Security system integration creates comprehensive home protection. When smart locks detect forced entry attempts, they immediately trigger security cameras to start recording, turn on all interior lights, and send emergency alerts to your smartphone. Motion sensors throughout the house can track intruder movement, and guide emergency responders to specific locations.

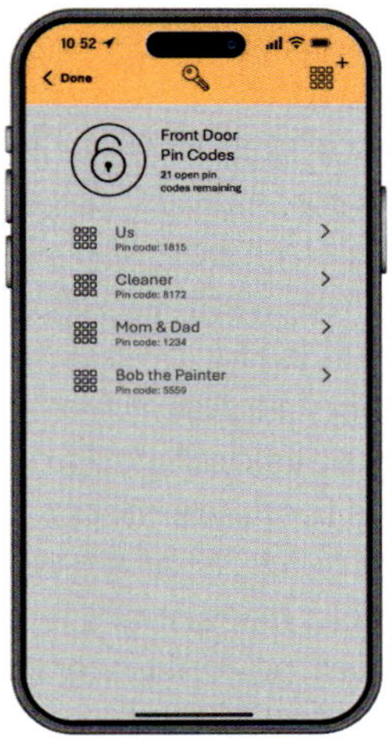

Smart outdoor lighting responds to security needs and energy efficiency goals. Motion-activated lights use AI to distinguish between legitimate activity and false triggers like swaying branches or passing cars. The systems learn your family's movement patterns, providing appropriate lighting without unnecessary activation. Pathway lights can create "lighting breadcrumbs" that illuminate safe routes from parking areas to entry doors.

Garden and outdoor smarts

Smart home AI now extends beyond your walls into gardens, lawns, and outdoor spaces. Weather-responsive irrigation systems and intelligent security devices create outdoor environments that maintain themselves while protecting your property.

Rachio Smart Sprinkler controllers revolutionize lawn and garden care through weather integration and soil monitoring. The systems connect to local weather services, automatically canceling scheduled watering when rain is forecast and adjusting schedules based on temperature, humidity, and seasonal changes.

Intelligent water management

Advanced irrigation AI considers multiple data sources: soil moisture sensors, plant types, sun exposure, and historical weather patterns. The system learns how different areas of your landscape respond to watering, developing customized schedules for flower beds, vegetable gardens, and grass areas. Deep-rooted trees might receive longer, less frequent watering, while shallow-rooted flowers get shorter, more frequent irrigation.

Water conservation happens automatically through intelligent scheduling. Smart irrigation systems apply water during optimal times—typically early morning when evaporation rates are lowest and wind speeds are minimal. The AI calculates precise watering durations based on soil absorption rates and plant requirements, preventing both underwatering and wasteful overwatering.

Seasonal adaptation ensures your landscape thrives year-round. Smart irrigation systems recognize that newly planted areas need more frequent watering, while established plants require less intensive care. The AI adjusts for seasonal plant needs, reducing watering frequency during dormant winter months and increasing support during active growing seasons.

Hot Tip

Smart irrigation systems can reduce outdoor water usage by 30-50% while keeping gardens healthier through consistent, optimized watering.

Weather integration and plant care

Smart outdoor devices watch weather forecasts and prepare automatically for changing conditions. Before a storm, smart awnings retract automatically, outdoor furniture covers deploy, and irrigation systems shut off to prevent overwatering. Wind sensors can trigger protective measures for delicate plants or outdoor decorations.

Plant care monitoring represents the cutting edge of garden AI. Smart sensors measure soil pH, nutrient levels, and moisture content, providing smartphone alerts when plants need attention.

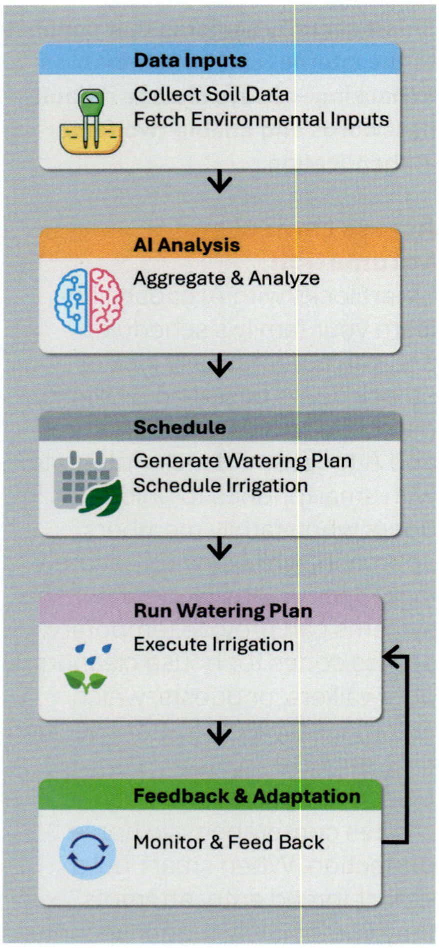

Some systems integrate with automatic fertilizer dispensers, maintaining optimal growing conditions without manual intervention. The Rachio 3 Smart Sprinkler Controller can even adjust watering schedules based on specific plant varieties and their unique water requirements.

Smart outdoor lighting extends security coverage while enhancing landscape aesthetics. Solar-powered LED lights with motion sensors can illuminate garden paths automatically while conserving energy during daylight hours. Advanced systems integrate with security cameras to provide additional lighting when suspicious activity is detected in outdoor areas.

Making it all work together

The real magic of smart homes happens when individual devices communicate and coordinate their actions. Instead of jumping between separate apps for your thermostat, lights, and security system, hubs like SmartThings, Apple Home, Home Assistant, and Hubitat connect everything into a unified system.

This integration creates seamless automation that feels genuinely intelligent. A "Goodnight" routine ensures all doors are locked, adjusts the thermostat, turns off lights, and arms the security system—all triggered by a single voice command. Leave for work, and your home automatically enters Away mode, adjusting temperatures and turning off unnecessary devices.

Creating unified automation

Smart home hubs learn your routine patterns and suggest automation improvements. If you consistently turn off the same three lights every night at 10:30 PM, the system will suggest creating an automated routine. Over time, these suggestions become more sophisticated, incorporating seasonal changes and special circumstances like vacations or house guests.

Voice control integration transforms how you interact with your home. Instead of reaching for light switches or thermostats, natural language commands handle multiple tasks simultaneously. "Hey Google, I'm going to bed" can dim lights throughout the house, lock all doors, set the security system, and adjust the thermostat to your preferred sleeping temperature.

Scene management allows you to create custom environmental settings for different activities. "Movie Night" might dim lights, close smart blinds, adjust the temperature to be slightly cooler, and switch the TV to your preferred streaming service. "Morning Routine" could gradually brighten lights, start the coffee maker, and provide weather updates for the day through your smart speaker.

Quick Start

Begin with two device automations before building complex scenarios—you'll discover what works best for your daily routine.

Advanced integration strategies

Cross-device communication enables sophisticated automation that feels almost magical. Your smart doorbell can trigger pathway lights when it detects a delivery truck, while simultaneously sending notifications to your smartphone and starting recording on security cameras. Motion sensors in your bedroom can signal the coffee maker to start brewing when you wake up earlier than usual.

Energy management integration optimizes your home's power consumption automatically. Smart thermostats communicate with solar panels and battery storage systems to use renewable energy when available, and shift power-hungry tasks to off-peak hours. Electric Vehicle chargers can coordinate with home energy systems to charge your car using excess solar power during sunny afternoons.

Seasonal automation adapts your entire home system for changing needs throughout the year. Winter settings might increase security camera sensitivity during longer nights while adjusting lighting schedules for shorter daylight hours. Summer automation could coordinate air conditioning with smart window shades to minimize cooling costs during peak heat hours.

The setup process for basic automation takes about five minutes using smartphone apps. Start with simple scenarios like "Bedtime" or "Away from Home" that coordinate just a few devices. Most successful smart home implementations grow gradually, adding devices and complexity over 6-12 months as you discover which automations genuinely improve your daily life.

Your next steps

Smart home transformation doesn't require wholesale replacement of every switch and appliance. The most successful implementations start with one device category and expand gradually over 6-12 months.

Begin with the area causing your biggest daily frustration. If you constantly adjust the thermostat, start there. If you forget to turn off lights, smart switches deliver immediate satisfaction. If you hate vacuuming, a robot vacuum provides obvious relief. Identify your household's biggest pain points and address those first.

Building your smart home strategy

Audit your current monthly utility bills before making purchases. Smart thermostats and lighting systems deliver measurable savings that help justify their costs. Energy Star's portfolio manager can help you track consumption changes after installing smart devices. Document your baseline energy usage so that you can measure the financial benefits of smart home investments.

Download relevant smartphone apps and explore automation options before expanding your system. Most smart home platforms offer free apps that demonstrate features and interface design. Spend time with one system before committing to additional devices. This exploration phase helps you understand which brands and interfaces work best for your family's technical comfort level.

Choose devices that work with multiple hub systems to avoid vendor lock-in. Products certified for SmartThings, HomeKit, and Alexa provide maximum flexibility for future expansion and integration with other smart home devices. This compatibility ensures your investment remains valuable even if you switch smart home platforms later. ■

Next Level

Plan your expansion around natural device replacement cycles—when your old thermostat fails, upgrade to a smart model rather than rushing to replace working equipment.

Voice assistants—make Siri, Alexa, and Google Assistant work for you

You asked a voice assistant for the weather this morning, set a timer while cooking lunch, or told it to play your favourite song. What you don't realize is that you're barely scratching the surface of what these digital helpers can do.

Most people use only a fraction of their voice assistant's capabilities, missing out on genuine time-savers and convenience features that will streamline their daily routines. While you're checking the weather manually on your phone, your voice assistant could be reading you a personalized morning briefing, adjusting your thermostat, and adding items to your shopping list—all before you've finished your first cup of coffee.

Getting the basics right

The difference between a frustrating voice assistant experience and a genuinely helpful one comes down to proper setup. Most people skip the initial configuration steps, then wonder why their assistant doesn't understand them or responds to the wrong person.

Voice training and profiles

Your assistant learns your speech patterns, accent, and pronunciation quirks—but only if you let it. Each major platform offers voice training that takes five minutes, and dramatically improves accuracy.

iPhone settings:

1. Settings app
2. **Siri & Search** option
3. Look for **"Hey Siri"** toggle
4. Set up **"Hey Siri"** button

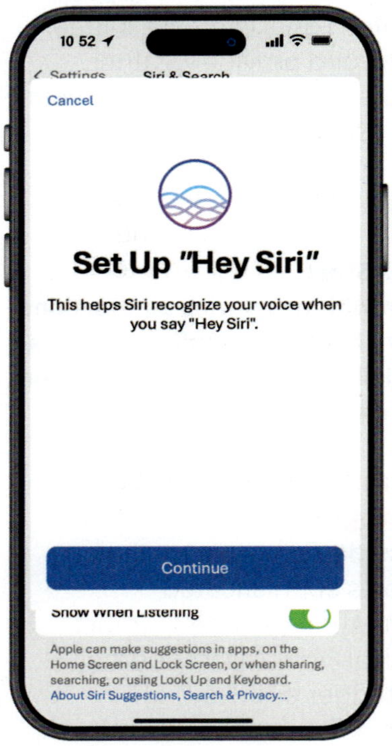

Google app settings:

1. Google app **More** tab
2. **Settings** menu
3. **Voice** section
4. **Voice Match** option
5. **Teach your Assistant your voice again** button

Alexa users can find voice training in the *Alexa* app:

1. Under **Settings**
2. Your **Profile**
3. **Voice**

Did You Know?
Your assistant learns your speech patterns—let each family member train their own voice profile.

The real game-changer is setting up household profiles. When your assistant knows who's talking, it provides personalized responses. Your teenager gets their Spotify playlist, while you get your preferred news source. Your partner's "Good Morning" routine turns on their preferred lighting, while yours starts the coffee maker.

Multiple users in one household need separate voice profiles. Without these set up, your assistant might read someone else's calendar or play the wrong music. Take 10 minutes to set up each family member—it prevents countless daily frustrations.

Effective command phrasing

Natural language processing has advanced significantly, but specific phrasing still gets better results. Instead of "Play music", try "Play my Discover Weekly playlist on Spotify". Rather than "Turn on the lights", say "Set the living room lights to 75%".

The key is being conversational but specific. Voice assistants excel at context when you give them enough information. "Schedule dinner with Mom for next Tuesday at 7" works better than a series of separate commands about calendars, contacts, and times.

Context matters for complex requests. "Add organic bananas to my Whole Foods shopping list" works better than just "Add bananas" when you shop at multiple stores. "Set a 20-minute timer for the lasagna" helps you remember what you're timing when multiple timers are running.

Troubleshooting common issues

Background noise wreaks havoc on voice recognition. Place smart speakers away from TVs, dishwashers, and air conditioning units. For phones, hold the device closer to your mouth in noisy environments or use the push-to-talk feature when available.

Accent issues often resolve with consistent use and voice training, but you can also adjust the assistant's language settings. Siri offers different English variants—American, British, Australian, Indian—while Google Assistant adapts to regional accents within the same language.

Warning
Review your voice history monthly—you might be surprised what's accidentally stored.

When your assistant stops responding correctly, restarting is often the solution. For smart speakers, unplug for 30 seconds and reconnect. For phones, restart the voice assistant app or toggle Siri/Google Assistant off and on in the settings.

Network connectivity affects response speed and accuracy. Voice assistants need stable internet connections to process commands in the cloud. Weak Wi-Fi signals cause delays and misunderstandings that frustrate users unnecessarily.

Beyond "Hey Siri, what's the weather?"

Once you've mastered the basics, voice assistants transform from novelty to necessity. The real power emerges when you integrate them into your smart home ecosystem and daily workflows.

Smart home control that makes sense

Voice control shines brightest with smart home devices. Saying "Goodnight" can lock doors, turn off lights, lower the thermostat, and arm your security system—all with a single command.

Start with lighting and temperature control. Smart bulbs and thermostats offer the biggest immediate impact. "Set bedroom lights to 10%" creates perfect ambiance for reading, while "Set temperature to 68 degrees" saves you from getting up to adjust the thermostat.

Security integration adds genuine convenience and peace

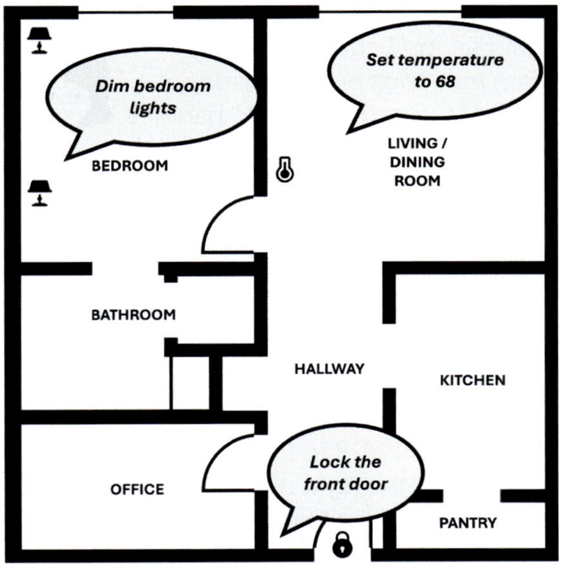

of mind. "Is the front door locked?" gives you instant confirmation, while "Show me the backyard camera" displays live footage on your smart display or phone.

Hot Tip
Smart thermostats can save you $180 annually on energy bills when voice-controlled for optimal scheduling.

Advanced users create seasonal routines. "Winter morning" adjusts heating higher and turns on bathroom floor warming, while "Summer evening" activates ceiling fans and closes smart blinds before the sun hits west-facing windows.

Calendar and task management

Voice assistants excel at calendar management because they understand natural language timing. "Schedule dentist appointment for next Thursday at 2 PM" creates an event and can send invites to family members who need to know about your schedule.

The real magic happens with recurring events and complex scheduling. "Schedule weekly team meetings every Tuesday at 10 AM starting next week" handles repetition automatically. "Move my 3 PM meeting to tomorrow" reschedules without opening apps or typing.

Location-based reminders work brilliantly through voice commands. "Remind me to buy milk when I'm at Target" uses your phone's GPS to trigger the reminder at the right place and time. "Remind me to call Mom when I leave work" activates based

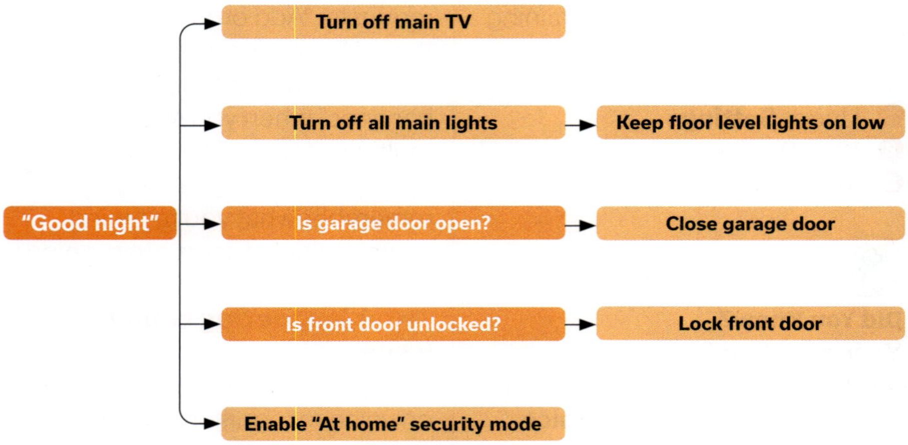

on your location changes.

Task management becomes effortless when you can capture thoughts instantly. "Add 'research new insurance rates' to my to-do list" records the task while you're driving or doing dishes. Voice assistants sync these tasks across all your devices automatically.

Shopping and lists that sync everywhere

Grocery lists become effortless when you can add items while cooking, cleaning, or doing other tasks. "Add Greek yogurt to my shopping list" captures the thought instantly, whether you're standing in the pantry or loading the dishwasher.

Voice assistants remember your purchase history and can reorder household essentials. "Reorder my usual coffee" works when you've established patterns. For Amazon Echo users, voice purchasing can automatically order frequently bought items with simple confirmations.

The synchronization across devices means everyone in your household can contribute. Your partner can add items from their phone while you're adding from the kitchen smart speaker, and everything appears on the same list.

Brand-specific requests work better than generic ones. "Add Tide laundry detergent to my Target list" ensures you get exactly what you want, while "Add laundry soap" might result in substitutions you don't want.

The power user's playbook

Advanced voice assistant features separate casual users from people who've genuinely integrated AI into their daily workflows. These capabilities require setup but deliver outsized convenience returns.

Custom routines that think ahead

Custom routines turn single phrases into complex sequences of actions. Your "Leaving Home" routine can lock doors, adjust the thermostat, turn off lights, and arm the security system. "Movie Time" dims lights, closes smart blinds, and starts your entertainment system.

The sophistication comes from conditional logic. Advanced routines can check the weather before deciding whether to water your garden or adjust based on time of day. Weekend morning routines differ from weekday versions automatically.

Siri Shortcuts, Google Routines, and Alexa Routines each offer different capabilities, but all can trigger multiple smart home devices, send messages, and run specific app functions with a single voice command.

Hot Tip

Power users create seasonal routines—"Winter Morning" adjusts heating and lighting differently from "Summer Morning".

Time-based conditions make routines smarter. "Good Morning" behaves differently at 6 AM versus 9 AM on weekends. Weather-based triggers adjust outdoor lighting and irrigation based on current conditions and forecasts.

Third-party integrations that expand possibilities

Voice assistants become even more useful when you connect them to third-party services. These connections—"skills" (Amazon), "actions" (Google), or "app integrations" (Apple)—help your assistant talk to other apps. Just as you download apps to add new functions to your phone, you enable "skills" to teach your assistant new tricks.

Banking skills let you check account balances and recent transactions with voice commands. "What's my checking account balance?" provides instant financial updates without opening apps.

Food delivery integrations let you reorder your usual restaurant meals without navigating menus. "Order my usual from Tony's Pizza" places your regular order automatically.

Uber and Lyft skills can request rides with destination and timing preferences you've established.

News briefings pull from multiple sources and customize based on your interests. Instead of generic headlines, you get updates on your local sports team, industry news, and specific topics you follow. Financial services provide portfolio updates and market summaries tailored to your investments.

Productivity integrations connect with task management apps like Todoist, project management tools like Asana, and note-taking apps like Evernote. "Add quarterly budget review to my work project" creates tasks in the right context automatically.

Warning

Curate your skills thoughtfully—too many installed skills create confusion and slower response times.

Cross-device coordination

The most seamless voice assistant experiences happen when your devices work together intelligently. Start a timer on your kitchen smart speaker, and it appears on your phone when you leave the house. Begin navigation on your phone, and it continues automatically when you get in your car.

Handoff between devices requires initial setup but creates remarkably fluid experiences. Your assistant can move music playback from your phone to your smart speaker when you arrive home, or from your speaker to your headphones when you head out for a run.

Multiple assistants can work together effectively. Your Amazon Echo might control smart home devices, while your iPhone handles calendar and messaging functions, creating a unified experience across different ecosystems.

When things go wrong

Even the best voice assistants have frustrating moments. The difference between giving up and becoming a power user often comes down to knowing how to troubleshoot effectively when technology doesn't cooperate.

Common problems and quick fixes

Your assistant stops responding to your voice commands, even though it worked perfectly yesterday. This usually means the microphone array needs cleaning or the device needs a simple restart. For smart speakers, unplug the power cord for 30 seconds, then reconnect. For phones, restart the voice assistant app or toggle the feature off and on in Settings.

Multiple devices responding to the same wake word creates chaos in multi-device households. Your phone, smart speaker, and tablet all try to answer "Hey Siri" simultaneously. Fix this by adjusting proximity settings—devices closer to your voice should take priority. In iPhone settings, enable "Automatic" for Siri responses, which uses sensors to determine which device you're addressing.

1. Tap on **Settings** > **Siri & Search**
2. Select the **Siri Responses** section
3. Select from **Automatic**, **Always On**, or **Hands-Free Only** options

Wrong music services playing despite your preferences happens when multiple family members link different accounts. Your "Play my music" command pulls from your teenager's Spotify instead of your Apple Music. Navigate to your assistant's settings and verify which music service is set as default for your voice profile specifically.

Smart home devices suddenly stop responding to voice commands while still working through their apps. This indicates a connectivity issue between your assistant and the smart home hub. Check your Wi-Fi network stability first, then re-discover devices through your assistant's smart home settings. For Alexa users, try "Alexa, discover my devices" to refresh connections.

Hot Tip

Most voice assistant problems resolve with the classic "turn it off and on again" approach—the tried-and-tested restart should fix 70+% of issues.

Calendar events going to the wrong person's schedule happens when household voice profiles aren't properly configured. Your dinner reservation gets added to your spouse's calendar instead of yours. Review voice recognition settings and ensure each family member has completed voice training for their individual profile.

The assistant volume suddenly being too quiet or too loud often relates to automatic volume adjustment features. Many devices adjust their speaking volume based on ambient noise or time of day. Check volume settings within your assistant's app—most platforms offer separate controls for responses, alarms, and media playback.

Getting help and resetting when all else fails

When basic troubleshooting doesn't work, each platform offers different support channels. Apple provides support through the Apple Support app, with chat and phone options for Siri issues. Schedule Genius Bar appointments for hardware-related problems with iPhones, iPads, or HomePods.

Google Assistant support operates through the Google Support website, with extensive troubleshooting guides and community forums. The Google Home app includes built-in help sections for device-specific issues. Live chat support is available for Google Nest hardware problems.

1. **Menu** button
2. **Help & Feedback** option
3. **Device troubleshooting** categories
4. **Contact Us** button
5. **Chat support** interface

Amazon offers the most comprehensive voice assistant support through multiple channels. The Alexa app includes extensive help documentation, while Amazon's customer service handles both software and hardware issues. Echo device problems often qualify for free replacements within their warranty periods.

Factory resetting becomes necessary when software corruption causes persistent problems. Before resetting, note down your custom routines, smart home device connections, and third-party skill preferences—you'll need to recreate these manually.

For smart speakers, locate the physical **Reset** button (usually on the bottom or back). Hold for 10-15 seconds until the light ring changes color or the device announces Reset mode. For phones, reset voice assistant settings through the main Settings menu without affecting other phone functions.

Warning

Back up your smart home device list and custom routines before factory resets—rebuilding from scratch takes hours.

Community forums provide solutions for unusual problems that official support channels haven't encountered. Reddit communities like *r/amazonecho*, *r/googlehome*, and *r/siri* offer user-generated solutions and

workarounds. These communities often identify widespread issues before official acknowledgment.

Re-linking accounts after connection problems requires specific steps for each service. Music streaming services occasionally disconnect and need manual re-authorization through your assistant's app. Smart home devices may require removing and re-adding to refresh authentication tokens.

When all troubleshooting fails, document the specific problem before contacting support. Note error messages, exact voice commands that aren't working, and which devices are affected. This information helps support representatives diagnose issues quickly, and provide targeted solutions.

Making it work for your life

The most successful voice assistant implementations align with your existing routines and genuine needs. Rather than forcing yourself to use every feature, focus on areas where voice control provides clear advantages over traditional methods.

Workplace productivity

Voice assistants excel at hands-free productivity tasks. "Set a 15-minute meeting timer" keeps discussions on track without checking your watch. "Take a note: Follow up with Jennifer about the quarterly report" captures thoughts without interrupting your workflow.

Quick calculations become effortless. "What's 347 times 23?" gets instant answers without reaching for a calculator app. Unit conversions, time zone calculations, and currency exchanges all work through natural voice commands.

Meeting preparation benefits from voice assistance. "What's on my calendar today?" provides a quick overview while you're getting coffee. "Call my 2 PM meeting" dials into conference calls automatically when you've set up the integration.

Hot Tip

Voice note-taking works best for capturing quick thoughts—longer content still requires typing.

Email management improves with voice commands. "Send a message to John saying I'll be five minutes late" handles quick communications while you're walking between meetings. Voice-to-text features work well for brief emails but struggle with complex formatting.

Family and household management

Children adapt to voice assistants quickly, and find them genuinely helpful for homework and entertainment. "How do you spell 'necessary'?" gets immediate answers during writing assignments. "What's 144 divided by 12?" helps with math homework without parents becoming human calculators.

Educational content ranges from multiplication tables to historical facts. "Tell me about the 'War of Independence'" provides age-appropriate information that can supplement school learning. Language learning features help with pronunciation and vocabulary building.

Bedtime routines work particularly well with voice control. "Play rain sounds for 30 minutes" creates soothing backgrounds for sleep. Storytelling features offer variety when you're tired of reading the same books repeatedly.

Timer functions help children develop time management skills. "Set a 20-minute cleanup timer" makes chores feel like games rather than endless tasks. Study timers help establish homework routines and break work into manageable chunks.

Seniors find voice assistants particularly valuable for aging in place independently. Medication reminders ensure important prescriptions aren't forgotten. "Remind me to take my blood pressure medication at 8 AM every day" creates reliable prompts. Check out the **AI for seniors** section on page 104 for more information on this.

Did You Know?
Voice control eliminates the need to navigate dark hallways or remember to secure the house for users with mobility challenges.

Emergency contact features offer peace of mind. Voice-activated calling to family members or emergency services provides safety nets when mobility is limited or during health emergencies.

Privacy and security essentials

Voice assistants record snippets of conversation to function, but you control more than you think. Most systems only record after hearing their wake word ("Hey Siri", "Alexa", "OK Google"), and you can review and delete these recordings regularly.

Regular privacy maintenance

takes a few minutes monthly. Check your voice history through each assistant's app or web interface. Delete recordings you don't want stored, and adjust privacy settings based on your comfort level.

The trade-off between convenience and privacy varies by person. More data sharing generally improves accuracy and personalization, but you can limit sharing while still getting most benefits.

Physical privacy matters too. Place smart speakers away from bedrooms and private conversation areas if you're concerned about accidental activation. **Mute** buttons provide instant privacy control when needed.

Guest mode settings let visitors use your devices without accessing your personal information. Most platforms offer temporary access that doesn't store guest interactions or provide access to your calendars and messages.

Your next steps

Voice assistants reward experimentation and gradual integration. Rather than trying to transform your entire routine overnight, focus on building sustainable habits around genuinely useful features.

This week, set up one new routine that addresses a current frustration. If you're always forgetting to lock your front door, create a "Goodnight" routine that handles it automatically.

Connect one smart home device that will provide immediate value. Explore three skills or actions you've never tried.

Review your privacy settings with fresh eyes. Understanding what's recorded and how it's used lets you make informed decisions about the trade-offs between convenience and privacy.

Start small, be patient with the learning curve, and focus on solving real problems rather than exploring every possible feature. Your voice assistant will become more valuable as you both learn to work together. ▪

Smarter photos–the AI in your phone's camera

Pro photographers have a saying for when they need to capture something in the moment: "The best camera is the one you have with you." Thanks to AI, the one in your pocket now shoots better pictures than most professionals' backup cameras.

Scene detection–your phone's hidden eye

Picture this: You're at your daughter's soccer game at dusk, the light fading fast. You pull out your phone, and somehow—without adjusting a single setting—you capture her mid-kick with perfect focus while the background melts into a gorgeous blur. Or you're on vacation, taking a selfie against a brilliant sunset that should wash out your face completely, yet you look magazine-perfect with the sky still glowing behind you.

This isn't luck. This isn't expensive equipment. This is AI doing the heavy lifting, turning every smartphone into a pocket-sized photo studio that would have cost thousands just a few years ago. Your camera already knows you're photographing food before you do.

How scene detection works

The moment you point your phone at that perfectly plated dinner, AI springs into action. Your device recognizes not just that you're taking a photo, but specifically what kind of photo you're taking. This happens through computer vision algorithms that analyze shapes, colors, textures, and lighting patterns in real time.

Your phone's AI has been trained on millions of photos across dozens of categories. It recognizes the curved edges and warm colors of food, the

geometric patterns of architecture, the organic shapes of flowers, and the movement patterns of pets. This training happens before you even buy the phone—the AI models are built into your phone's camera app. The processing happens in milliseconds, completely behind the scenes. The AI analyzes the image before you even press the shutter, adjusting exposure, color balance, focus points, and even shutter speed based on what it "sees".

Common scene types your phone recognizes

Modern phones can instantly identify dozens of different scenarios. Food gets warmer tones and enhanced texture to make that pasta look as delicious as it tastes. Pets get faster focus tracking because the AI knows they won't sit still. Landscapes get deeper colors and sharper details to capture those vacation vistas. Documents get contrast boosting and perspective correction for readable scans.

An iPhone automatically switches to Macro mode when you get within a few inches of your subject—perfect for close-up flower photography. Google's camera activates Night Sight the moment it detects low-light conditions. Samsung's Scene Optimizer tweaks settings for everything from beaches to babies, with over 30 distinct scene types.

Beach photos get enhanced blues and reduced glare. Concert photos get noise reduction and better low-light performance. Snow scenes get exposure compensation to keep white snow looking white instead of gray. Text documents get automatic perspective correction and contrast enhancement for perfect scanning.

Did You Know?

Your phone can identify specific dog breeds and adjust focus tracking accordingly—Golden Retrievers get different settings than Chihuahuas.

The best part? You never have to remember which mode to use. No more blurry dinner photos for Instagram because you forgot to switch from Landscape to Food mode.

Portrait mode–the professional studio in your pocket

That gorgeous, blurred background used to require a $2,000 lens. Professional photographers spent years learning how to achieve that perfect shallow Depth of Field effect—the one where your subject pops against a beautifully blurred background. They invested in expensive cameras with large sensors and fast lenses, then mastered complex manual settings to nail the shot every time.

Now, your phone creates the same stunning look using pure computational photography—no experience required. The AI analyzes your scene, identifies your subject, and applies professional-grade effects instantly. What once demanded thousands of dollars in equipment and years of training now happens with a simple tap on your screen.

Understanding depth mapping technology

Professional photographers call it "bokeh"—that creamy, out-of-focus background that makes portrait subjects pop. For decades, achieving this effect meant carrying expensive cameras with large sensors and fast lenses. Now, your phone creates the same look using pure computational photography.

Here's how the magic happens: Your phone takes multiple photos simultaneously, using different lenses or advanced sensor techniques to map the depth of everything in the frame. The AI creates a detailed 3D map of your scene, measuring how far away each pixel is from the camera. It then identifies your subject (usually a person's face and shoulders) and artificially blurs everything else based on distance.

Different manufacturers use varying approaches. iPhones with multiple lenses work together, comparing slightly different perspectives to calculate depth. Google Pixel phones rely heavily on Machine Learning trained on millions of portrait photos, using a single lens but sophisticated software. Samsung phones often combine dedicated depth sensors with AI processing for enhanced accuracy.

Portrait mode across different phones

Each brand has developed its own strengths. Google excels at edge detection around challenging areas like hair and glasses, where traditional depth sensing struggles. Its AI has learned to recognize these tricky boundaries through extensive training. Apple delivers the most natural-looking blur gradation, mimicking how expensive camera lenses actually behave. Samsung offers the most control, letting you adjust blur intensity even after taking the shot.

The technology keeps improving with each generation. Early Portrait modes struggled with

glasses, curly hair, and complex backgrounds like chain-link fences. Today's AI handles these challenging scenarios with impressive accuracy, though you'll still occasionally spot telltale signs of computational photography—like a slightly soft ear or an overly sharp background detail that the AI missed.

Even budget phones now deliver professional-looking portraits. What once required thousands of dollars in equipment now happens with a tap of your screen. The Pixel 7a produces portraits that rival phones costing twice as much, thanks to Google's advanced AI processing.

Hot Tip

Portrait mode works best when your subject is 2-8 feet away—too close, and the depth mapping gets confused; too far, and facial features become too small to detect properly.

Night photography–seeing in the dark

AI turns your phone into a vampire—it sees perfectly in the dark. For decades, night photography separated amateur snap-shooters from serious photographers. The technical challenges were immense: balancing ISO sensitivity against image noise, calculating exposure times that wouldn't blur moving subjects, and managing the harsh trade-offs between available light and image quality.

Most people simply avoided taking photos after sunset, knowing they'd end up with grainy, blurry disappointments or harshly lit flash shots that flattened every subject. Professional night photography required expensive equipment, tripods, and extensive post-processing skills that put great low-light images out of reach for casual photographers.

Multi-frame processing magic

Remember when taking photos at night meant choosing between grainy, noisy shots or harsh, unflattering flash? Those days are over. Modern smartphones can now capture stunning images in conditions that would challenge dedicated cameras.

The secret is multi-frame processing powered by Machine Learning. When you activate Night mode, your phone doesn't take just one photo—it captures between 3 and 15 shots over several seconds, each with different settings. Some frames prioritize bright areas, others focus on shadow detail, and still others capture color information. AI then combines these images intelligently, keeping the sharp details while reducing noise and brightening shadows. The processing identifies which parts of each frame are sharpest, and combines them into a single, perfectly exposed image. Motion detection algorithms compensate for slight hand movement between frames.

When Night mode activates

Google pioneered this technology with Night Sight, which can literally photograph scenes that look pitch-black to your eyes. Apple's Night mode automatically activates in low light, holding the shutter

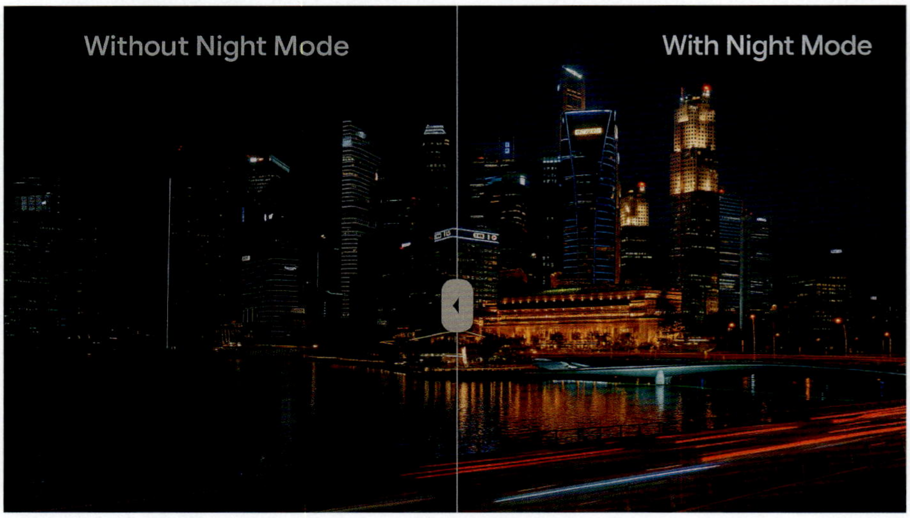

longer to gather more photons. Samsung's Bright Night mode combines multiple techniques, including AI-powered noise reduction and intelligent exposure bracketing.

The AI does more than just brighten the image. It identifies different elements—sky, buildings, people, vegetation—and processes each separately. Streets get detail enhancement without looking artificial. Skies remain naturally dark instead of being brightened into an unnatural gray. Faces get gentle brightening without the ghostly appearance of traditional flash photography.

There are still limits to what physics allows. Moving subjects can appear ghostly or doubled if they shift during the multi-second capture. Extremely bright lights like car headlights might still create flares. And you absolutely need to hold steady—any camera shake during the capture will blur your results, no matter how sophisticated the AI processing.

Warning

Night mode requires holding perfectly still for 2-3 seconds—even slight movement can ruin the shot. Use a tripod or brace against a wall for best results.

Hold steady for those few seconds, and get results that look like daylight photography—but with that magical nighttime atmosphere perfectly intact.

Smart HDR–balancing the impossible

Remember squinting into the sun for family photos? AI fixed that. High Dynamic Range (HDR) photography tackles one of the

most frustrating problems in everyday photography: scenes where some parts are too bright and others are too dark. Think about every family vacation photo where you had to choose between seeing people's faces or preserving that gorgeous sunset backdrop.

Traditional cameras forced impossible decisions. Expose for the bright sky, and your family disappears into silhouettes. Expose for people's faces, and the beautiful scenery behind them becomes a washed-out white blob. Professional photographers spent years learning complex techniques like exposure bracketing and graduated neutral density filters to solve this problem—techniques that required expensive equipment and considerable skill.

When HDR activates automatically

HDR photography solves one of photography's oldest problems: scenes with both very bright and very dark areas. Think family photos on a sunny beach, where faces are either too dark or the sky is blown out white. Traditional cameras had to choose—expose for the faces and lose the sky, or capture the scenery and lose the people.

Smart HDR takes multiple photos at different exposures faster than you can blink. One shot captures detail in the shadows (your family's faces). Another preserves the bright areas (that gorgeous sky). A third might focus on mid-tone details. AI then combines them intelligently, creating a single image that shows detail everywhere.

This happens automatically on modern phones. The moment your camera detects high contrast—like shooting indoors near a bright window—HDR kicks in without any input from you. The processing is so fast you won't even notice the multiple exposures, except that your photos suddenly look much better.

HDR vs. standard photography

Different scenarios benefit from smart HDR in different ways. Beach photos keep both sand details and cloud textures visible. Indoor shots near windows show people clearly without washing out the view outside. Sunset portraits capture both the golden sky and your subject's face perfectly—something that was nearly impossible with traditional photography.

The technology has become sophisticated enough to handle moving subjects too. Early HDR created ghosting effects when people moved between the different exposures. Today's AI can identify and compensate for motion, keeping everything sharp while still balancing the exposure perfectly.

Modern HDR processing also includes tone mapping—adjusting the overall contrast and color saturation to look natural rather than over-processed. The AI has learned what realistic photos should look like, avoiding the artificial "HDR look" that plagued earlier implementations.

Warning
HDR can sometimes make photos look overly processed with unnatural colors—most phones let you turn it off in the Camera app's settings if you prefer more natural results.

What once required careful manual camera work and expensive post-processing software now happens instantly, every time you press the shutter.

Object removal and enhancement–the magic eraser

That photobomber just vanished—and you didn't need Photoshop. For years, removing unwanted elements from photos required expensive software, hours of learning complex tools, and considerable artistic skill. Professional photo editors charged hundreds of dollars to seamlessly remove objects from important images, because the work was so technically demanding.

Even basic edits like removing a trash can from a scenic landscape or erasing strangers from a family photo meant mastering layers, clone stamps, and healing brushes in programs that intimidated most casual photographers. The results often looked obviously edited, with telltale signs of digital manipulation that screamed "fake" to anyone who looked closely.

Magic Eraser and similar tools

The latest AI camera features move beyond traditional photography into the realm of computational magic. Google's Magic Eraser lets you tap on unwanted objects—strangers walking through your shot, power lines cutting across a landscape, trash cans in a scenic view—and watch them disappear. The AI fills in the gaps so seamlessly you'd never know they were there.

Samsung's Object Eraser works similarly, while also offering features like sky replacement and automatic color enhancement. Point at a dull, gray sky in your photo, and the AI can swap it for a more dramatic sunset or a clear blue sky that matches the lighting in your scene perfectly.

Apple's Clean Up feature on iPhones with Apple Intelligence also allows you to remove unwanted objects and people from photos. It seamlessly blends in the background where the object or person used to be, making the edit look completely natural.

These features work by understanding context through advanced Machine Learning. The AI analyzes the surrounding area and intelligently predicts what should be there. A person standing in front of a brick wall gets replaced with more brick wall that matches the existing pattern. Someone blocking part of a sunset gets replaced with more sunset, complete with appropriate colors and gradients that blend naturally.

Real-time vs. post-processing features

Some phones offer real-time object removal, letting you see the effect before you even take the photo. Point your camera at a scene, and distracting elements simply vanish from your viewfinder. This preview shows you exactly what your final photo will look like, letting you compose the shot perfectly.

Post-processing removal happens after you've taken the photo, giving you more time to carefully select exactly what to remove. This approach often delivers better results because the AI has more processing time and can use more sophisticated algorithms.

The results aren't always perfect—complex textures and detailed backgrounds can sometimes look obviously edited. Removing objects from busy scenes like crowded markets or dense forests

remains challenging. But for simple removals against clean backgrounds, the technology is remarkably effective.

What once required expensive software like Photoshop, and considerable skill, now happens with a few taps on your phone screen. The democratization of advanced photo editing puts professional-level tools in everyone's pocket.

Hot Tip

Object removal works best on simple, repeating backgrounds like sky, water, or walls—complex textures may show obvious editing artifacts.

AI video features motion picture magic

Your phone's AI doesn't just enhance photos—it's revolutionizing video too. While smartphone photography grabbed headlines for challenging professional cameras, video remained the domain of expensive equipment and specialized skills. Creating smooth, cinematic footage required gimbal stabilizers, manual focus pulling, and careful planning that put Hollywood-style results out of reach for most people.

Recording anything beyond basic home movies meant investing in additional gear and learning complex techniques. Shaky handheld footage looked amateurish. Keeping subjects in focus while they moved required constant attention and practice. Even simple effects like smooth focus transitions between subjects demanded equipment that cost more than most people's entire camera budget.

Cinematic mode and Depth of Field

Apple's Cinematic mode brings Hollywood-style focus effects to smartphone video. Just like Portrait mode for photos, it creates that professional shallow Depth of Field look where your subject stays sharp while the background blurs beautifully. But here's the clever part: it can automatically shift focus between subjects as they move around the frame.

The AI tracks faces and predicts where attention should be focused. When someone new enters the conversation, focus smoothly transitions to them. When they look at another person, the camera follows their gaze and shifts focus accordingly. It's like having an intelligent camera operator making creative decisions in real time.

Samsung's Director's View takes a different approach, letting you switch between multiple camera angles while recording. The AI helps stabilize each view, and can even suggest the most interesting perspective based on what's happening in the scene.

Action mode and stabilization

Google's Action Mode and Apple's Action mode use AI-powered stabilization to smooth out incredibly shaky footage. Whether you're running, biking, or just walking while filming, the AI analyzes motion patterns and compensates for camera shake in ways that traditional optical stabilization can't match.

The technology works by cropping into the image slightly, and using AI to predict and counteract movement. It's like having a professional gimbal built into your phone, but without the bulk and expense.

Next Level

Action mode works best in good lighting—low light reduces the AI's ability to track motion patterns effectively.

Built-in editing and enhancement–your personal photo assistant

AI doesn't stop working after you take the photo—it continues improving your images automatically. Traditional photo editing meant opening separate apps, learning complex tools, and spending considerable time adjusting exposure, color balance, and contrast manually. Even basic improvements like brightening a dark photo or enhancing dull colors required understanding technical concepts that intimidated many casual photographers.

Professional photo editors developed their skills over years, learning to recognize what makes images pop, and mastering the subtle adjustments that transform ordinary shots into compelling photos. Most people either skipped editing entirely or applied heavy-handed filters that made their photos look obviously processed and artificial.

Automatic enhancement suggestions

Modern phones analyze every photo you take, and offer intelligent enhancement suggestions. The AI might suggest brightening a slightly dark photo, enhancing colors in a landscape, or adjusting the crop for better composition. These aren't random adjustments—they're based on analyzing millions of professionally edited photos.

Google Photos' auto-enhance

feature can dramatically improve photos with a single tap. It analyzes the image and applies multiple adjustments simultaneously—exposure correction, color balancing, highlight recovery, and shadow lifting—all calibrated to work together naturally.

Apple's photo-editing suggestions appear as small icons below your images, indicating what improvements the AI recommends. Tap one, and see an instant preview of the enhancement. Don't like it? Tap again to remove it.

Smart cropping and straightening

AI can identify the most interesting parts of your photos and suggest better crops automatically. It recognizes faces, horizon lines, and points of interest, then recommends crops that follow photographic composition rules like the Rule of Thirds.

Auto-straightening uses horizon detection to fix tilted photos instantly. The AI identifies horizontal and vertical lines in your image—like buildings, horizons, or architecture—and adjusts the rotation to make them perfectly level.

Did You Know?

AI crop suggestions are based on analyzing composition patterns from millions of award-winning photographs.

Photo organization and search–finding needles in digital haystacks

AI transforms your photo library from a chaotic mess into an organized, searchable database. Most people have thousands of photos scattered across their devices—family gatherings mixed with screenshots, vacation memories buried between random snapshots, and important moments lost in an endless scroll of digital clutter. Finding a specific photo meant scrolling for minutes or even hours through chronological feeds that offered no helpful organization.

Traditional photo management required manual effort that nobody had time for. Creating albums meant selecting photos one by one and remembering to categorize them consistently. Tagging people required typing names repeatedly. Searching meant remembering approximate dates or scrolling endlessly through camera rolls that grew larger every day, turning photo libraries into digital graveyards where precious memories disappeared into the chaos.

Facial recognition and people albums

Your phone's AI automatically identifies and groups photos of the same people, creating personal albums without any manual tagging. The technology recognizes faces across different ages, lighting conditions, and even partial views. It can identify someone from childhood photos through to recent pictures, accounting for natural changes in appearance.

The AI also learns relationships, grouping family members and friends who frequently appear together. It can even identify pets and create albums for your furry family members.

Privacy controls let you manage this feature completely. You can remove someone from facial recognition, merge incorrectly separated albums, or turn off the feature entirely. All processing happens on your device—facial recognition data never leaves your phone.

Smart search and auto-generated albums

Search your photos using natural language like "beach vacation 2023" or "photos with John at restaurants". The AI understands the context and content of your images, not just metadata like dates and locations.

Auto-generated albums appear based on events, trips, or themes the AI detects. It might create a "Weekend in Chicago" album by recognizing location patterns and timing, or a "First Steps" album by identifying similar photos of a toddler learning to walk.

Hot Tip

Use specific search terms like "sunset", "birthday cake", or "dog park" to find photos faster than scrolling through thousands of images.

The AI continues learning your preferences, getting better at creating relevant albums and understanding your search intentions over time.

Lenses that actually matter–when hardware meets AI

That $30 clip-on lens might be the smartest photography investment you'll make.

While phone cameras have evolved dramatically, not everyone has the latest flagship device with multiple built-in lenses. If you're using an older phone or want to push beyond what even the newest models can capture, a well-chosen add-on lens can dramatically expand your creative possibilities—especially when paired with AI processing.

Choosing the right add-on lenses

The key words here are "well-chosen". The mobile photography accessory market is flooded with gimmicky filters and fisheye lenses that deliver novelty shots you'll never use. Focus on two types that actually matter: wide-angle and macro lenses.

Wide-angle lenses let you capture more of the scene—perfect for group photos, architecture, or landscapes where you can't step back far enough. Your phone's AI will still handle scene detection, HDR processing, and automatic adjustments. In fact, some AI features work even better with more visual information to process.

Macro lenses open up an entirely new world of close-up photography. While some newer phones have dedicated macro cameras built in, add-on macro lenses often deliver superior image quality and work with older devices. Your phone's AI will still optimize focus and exposure, but now you can capture intricate details that were impossible before.

Brand recommendations and AI compatibility

The premium option is Moment lenses, which offer exceptional optical quality and seamless integration with most phones. SANDMARC provides excellent middle-ground options with solid build quality. For budget-conscious photographers, Amazon offers surprisingly capable options starting at around $20—just read reviews carefully and stick with highly rated products.

PHONE CAMERA

CLIP-ON MACRO LENS

Here's a reality check: some AI features may not work perfectly with add-on lenses. Portrait mode's depth sensing can get confused by the optical changes. Some automatic scene detection might not trigger correctly. But basic AI processing—HDR, noise reduction, color optimization—continues to work just fine.

Hot Tip
Clean both your phone lens AND the add-on lens—double the smudge risk, double the cleaning needs.

Skip the fisheye gimmicks and dramatic filter effects. Wide-angle and macro lenses deliver actual value that you'll use regularly, not just for novelty shots.

Tripods, lights, and grips–the support system

Even AI can't fix camera shake when you're shooting your kid's graduation from the bleachers.

AI has solved many photography problems, but physics isn't one of them. Camera shake still ruins photos, especially in low light when your phone needs longer exposures. Poor lighting still creates harsh shadows and unflattering portraits. And holding your phone steady for group photos while running around to get in the shot remains awkward.

This is where simple, inexpensive accessories can dramatically improve your results—not by replacing AI features, but by giving them better conditions to work with.

Stability solutions for AI photography

Start with stability. A compact tripod or phone grip makes an enormous difference for Night mode photography. Remember—night shots require your phone to hold the shutter open for several seconds while combining multiple exposures. Any hand movement during this process will blur your results, no matter how sophisticated the AI processing.

Mini tripods that fit in your pocket cost as little as $15 and work with any phone. Phone grips—rings or handles that attach to your device—provide steadier handheld shooting, and reduce the risk of drops. For serious video work, gimbal stabilizers smooth out movement that even AI stabilization can't fully correct.

Lighting and remote control accessories

Lighting accessories work beautifully with AI Portrait modes. Instead of the harsh built-in flash that AI often struggles to balance, portable LED light panels provide even, controllable illumination. Your phone's AI will still handle background blur and skin tone optimization, but now it has quality light to work with.

The key is choosing LED lights with good color temperature ratings. Cheap lights can throw off your phone's white balance AI, creating unnatural skin tones that are hard to correct. Look for panels that offer both warm and cool light settings, typically marked as "bi-color" or showing a temperature range like 3200K-5600K.

Warning

Cheap LED lights can mess with AI white balance—look for adjustable color temperature settings to avoid unnatural skin tones.

Wireless shutter releases solve the group photo problem elegantly. Bluetooth remotes let you set up your shot, get in position, and trigger the camera without the awkward timer sprint. Many also work with your phone's voice commands so that you can simply say "take a photo" once everything's positioned.

Getting started with AI photography

Your best photos aren't ahead of you—they're in your pocket right now.

Essential settings to check

Ready to unlock your phone's full photographic potential? Start by optimizing your camera settings for AI features.

First, update your phone's Camera app. Many AI features require the latest version of your phone's camera software. Check your app store for updates, and don't ignore those system updates that often include camera improvements.

Next, review the Camera app's settings to ensure AI features are enabled. Most phones default to Automatic modes, but it's worth checking:

1. **Turn on automatic HDR** if it's not already enabled
2. **Enable scene detection** for automatic photo optimization
3. **Activate automatic Night mode** for low-light situations
4. **Check Portrait mode settings** and depth effect options
5. **Enable photo suggestions** for AI-powered editing recommendations

Clean your lens while you're at it. AI can enhance your photos in incredible ways, but it can't fix smudges on your camera lens. A quick wipe with a soft cloth will instantly improve every photo you take.

Your first AI photography projects

Now for the fun part—putting these AI features to work:

Week 1: Try Night mode. Wait until evening, and photograph the same scene with and without Night mode. You'll be amazed at what your phone can capture in seemingly impossible lighting conditions.

Week 2: Experiment with Portrait mode. Take portraits of family members, pets, and even objects. Notice how the AI handles different subjects and backgrounds.

Week 3: Test scene detection. Photograph food, landscapes, documents, and pets. Watch how your phone automatically adjusts settings for each scenario.

Week 4: Explore object removal. Use Magic Eraser or similar features to clean up photos you've already taken. Remove distracting elements from your favorite shots.

Quick Start

Pick one AI feature this week and use it daily—you'll master it faster through regular practice than with occasional experimentation.

Your phone's camera already knows how to take better photos than most people realize. The only thing left is to let it show you what it can do. ■

Deep dive

Roll up your sleeves–and prepare to get hands-on experience of working with some common tools.

Meet your new chatty friends–getting creative with generative AI

You're staring at a blank email to your landlord about that broken dishwasher, searching for the right tone between polite and firm. 10 minutes later, you're still typing and deleting the same opening line.

What if you could describe your situation in plain English to a digital writing partner and get three different versions of that email—professional, friendly, or assertive—in 30 seconds?

That's generative AI in action, and it's already waiting for you: on your phone, your tablet, and even in the web browser on your computer.

Why these AI tools feel like conversations

Unlike search engines that hunt down existing web pages, generative AI creates something new just for you. Think of it as the difference between hiring a researcher who brings you stacks of other people's work versus hiring a writer who crafts original content based on your specific needs.

When you type a question into Google, it searches billions of web pages to find ones that might contain your answer. When you type that same question into ChatGPT, Claude, or another generative AI, rather than just running a search it generates a response tailored specifically to your question, written in that moment just for you.

Three game-changing capabilities

This fundamental difference opens up three game-changing capabilities. First, these AIs write—everything from emails and essays to poems and code. Second, they reason through problems, breaking down complex situations into manageable steps. Third, they solve creative challenges, generating ideas and approaches you might never have considered.

Real examples make this clearer. Need to draft a delicate email to HR about a workplace issue? Describe the situation to an AI and get back professional language that strikes the right balance. Struggling to understand your medical insurance paperwork? Upload the text and receive a plain-English explanation. Planning a dinner party for guests with conflicting dietary restrictions? Get a complete menu with recipes that keep everyone happy.

Hot Tip

Unlike search engines that search and return existing content, generative AI creates original responses tailored to your specific needs.

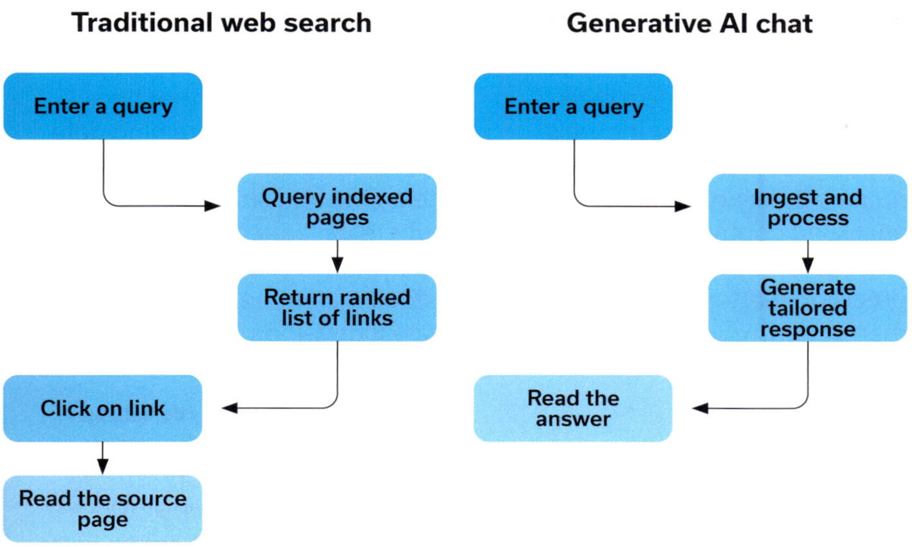

Five minutes that could save you hours

Let's get specific about how generative AI transforms everyday frustrations into quick wins. These aren't theoretical examples or marketing promises—they're real situations where AI delivers immediate, practical value.

The beauty of generative AI lies in its ability to tackle the small, time-consuming tasks that eat away at your day. You know the ones: staring at blank screens, struggling with tone in important emails, or spending hours researching something that should take minutes.

Real problems, real solutions

The Stuck Writer: You need to write a thank-you note to your child's teacher but can't find the right words. Tell the AI: "Help me write a sincere thank-you note to my daughter's third-grade teacher who stayed late three times this month to help with her reading." In seconds, you'll have a heartfelt message that captures exactly what you wanted to say.

The Overwhelmed Parent: The school just sent home a 15-page policy document about the new grading system. Instead of struggling through education jargon, upload it to Claude and ask: "Summarize this grading policy in simple bullet points, focusing on what parents need to know." You'll get the key information in a format you can actually use.

From stuck to unstuck

The Career Changer: You're thinking about transitioning from retail to digital marketing but don't know where to start. Ask for a personalized learning plan: "I have 10 years of retail experience and want to move into digital marketing. Create a 6-month self-study plan using free resources." You'll receive a structured roadmap with specific courses, skills to develop, and projects to build your portfolio.

The Small Business Owner: You've taken product photos but need compelling descriptions for your online store. Upload an image and say: "Write 3 different product descriptions for this handmade ceramic mug—one focused on gift-giving, one on sustainability, and one on the artisan craftsmanship." Transform one photo into multiple marketing angles.

Beyond the basics

The Curious Mind: Your teenager asks about cryptocurrency over dinner, and you want to give an informed answer without sounding clueless. Request: "Explain cryptocurrency to me like I'm a smart adult who's never really understood it, then give me a simpler version I can share with my 14-year-old." Get explanations calibrated to exactly the right level.

The Problem Solver: You're dealing with a difficult neighbor

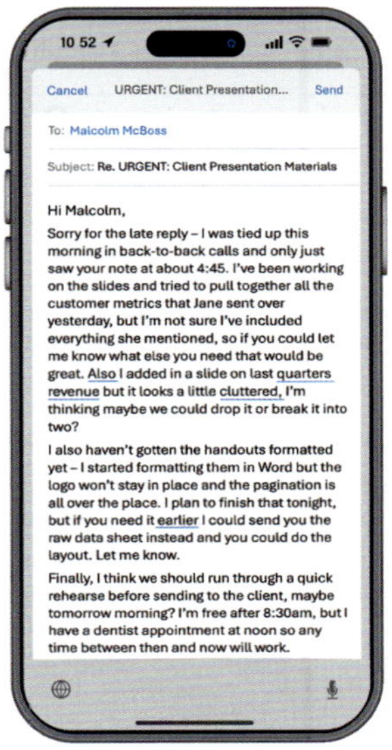

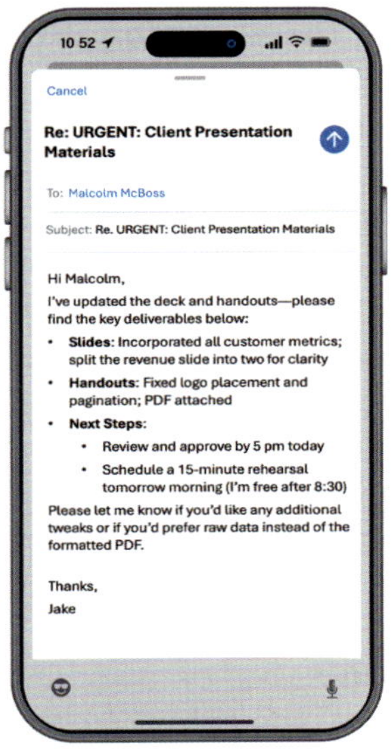

situation and need to approach it diplomatically. Describe the issue and ask: "Help me draft a conversation outline for addressing noise complaints with my neighbor that maintains a good relationship while solving the problem." Get a structured approach that considers both perspectives.

Quick Start
Try this right now—pick any writing task you've been putting off and describe it to an AI in plain English.

Meet your new digital assistants

Three major players dominate the generative AI landscape, each with its own personality and strengths. Understanding their differences helps you pick the right tool for each task.

Think of it like choosing the right person for different jobs. You wouldn't ask the same friend to help you move furniture, plan your wedding, and review your tax returns—each requires different skills and approaches. The same principle applies to AI tools.

The big three personalities

ChatGPT feels like chatting with a knowledgeable friend who's great at brainstorming. Ask it to help you write a wedding toast, debug some code, or explain quantum physics using only food metaphors, and it delivers with personality. It's the Swiss Army knife of AI—versatile enough for creative writing, analytical enough for research, and patient enough to work through problems step by step.

Claude is your detail-oriented colleague who actually reads the fine print. Upload a 50-page employee handbook, and Claude will turn it into a clear, actionable summary. It excels at understanding context and nuance, making it perfect for analyzing contracts, research papers, or any situation where precision matters much more than speed.

Perplexity is like having a research librarian who never sleeps. Unlike the other two, which rely on their training data, Perplexity searches the web in real time and shows you exactly where each piece of information comes from. Ask about yesterday's stock market performance or the latest developments in renewable

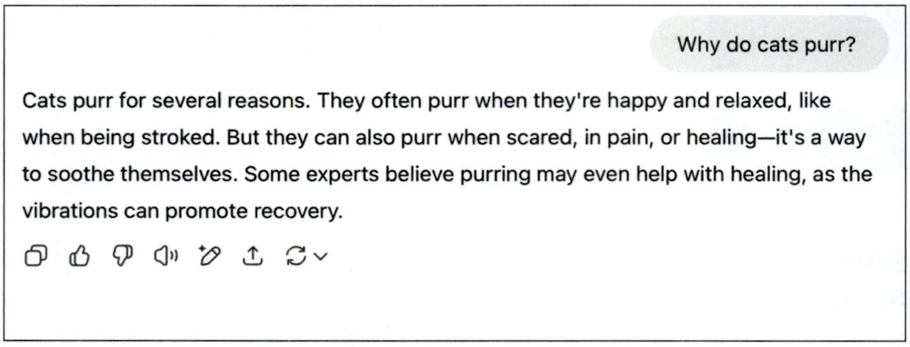

ChatGPT

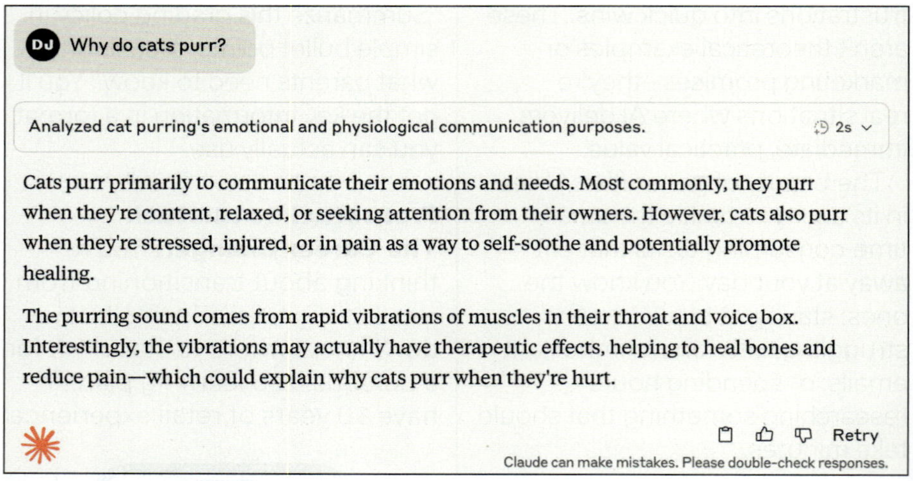

Claude

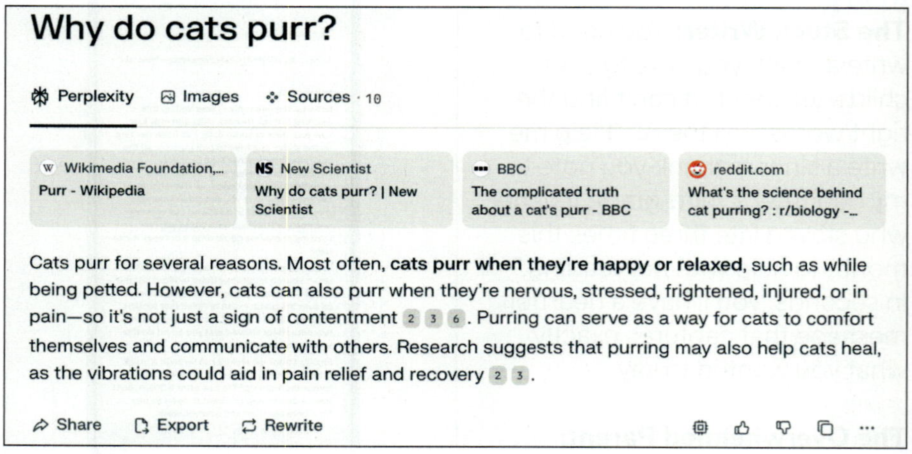

Perplexity

energy, and you'll get current information with clickable sources.

Did You Know?
ChatGPT can remember context from earlier in your conversation, so you can build on previous responses without repeating yourself.

Matching tools to tasks

All three share core capabilities. They draft and edit text, explain concepts at any level, translate languages, generate ideas and solutions, and even code simple programs. The magic lies in how they approach these tasks.

Use ChatGPT when you want to bounce ideas around, need creative help, or want an AI that can handle multiple tasks in one conversation. It's particularly strong at maintaining context across long discussions and adapting its tone to match your needs.

Use Claude when you're working with documents, need careful analysis, or want responses that feel more measured and thoughtful. It's the best choice for turning complex information into something digestible.

Use Perplexity when you need current information, want to verify facts, or need to know where your answers are coming from. It's invaluable for research, staying updated on recent events, or any time-source credibility matters.

Warning
Each AI has different strengths, so trying multiple tools for the same task often yields better results.

"The best AI tool is the one that matches your thinking style for each specific task."

Getting started without commitment

You don't need to pick just one. Many people use ChatGPT for creative projects, Claude for document work, and Perplexity for research. Each has a free tier that lets you experiment before committing to paid plans.

Getting started requires minimal setup. All three offer web-based access without downloads. ChatGPT and Claude require simple account creation, while Perplexity works immediately without signing up—though creating an account unlocks additional features.

These aren't just different brands of the same product. They're genuinely different tools optimized for different types of thinking and working. ChatGPT excels at creative collaboration, Claude specializes in careful analysis, and Perplexity dominates real-time research with verified sources.

Next Level
Advanced users can chain prompts together—use one AI's output as input for another tool to get even more refined results.

Hot Tip
Other generative AI tools are being released or updated all the time.

How to talk to AI (it's easier than you think)

The secret to getting great results from AI lies in how you ask. Think of it like giving directions to a helpful friend—the clearer you are about where you're starting and where you want to go, the better they can help you get there.

Many people approach AI like they're talking to a search engine, typing short keywords and hoping for the best. But generative AI works more like a conversation with a thoughtful colleague who needs context to give you exactly what you need.

The three-part formula

The basic formula has three parts. First, set the context by explaining who you are or what situation you're in. Then, define the task clearly. Finally, specify what kind of output you want.

Here's how it works in practice. Instead of typing "Write an email demanding payment", try: "I'm a small business owner who hasn't been paid for a project completed two months ago. Help me write a professional but firm email requesting immediate payment that maintains the relationship but makes clear this delay is unacceptable." It's longer, and can feel awkward, like you're chatting with a robot butler, but the effort makes for much better results.

Starter prompts that work

Try these three starter prompts with any AI tool:

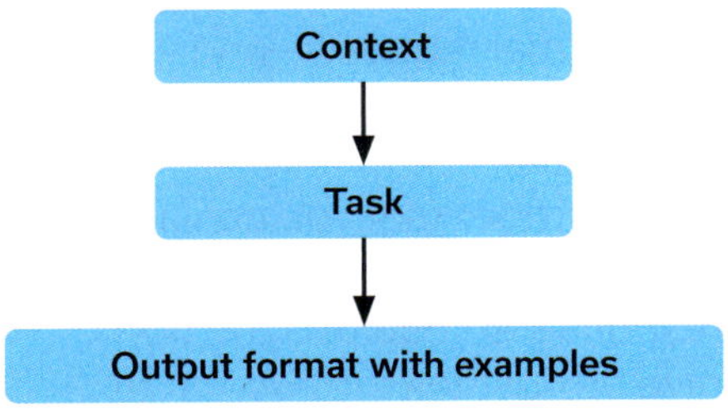

ChatGPT interface

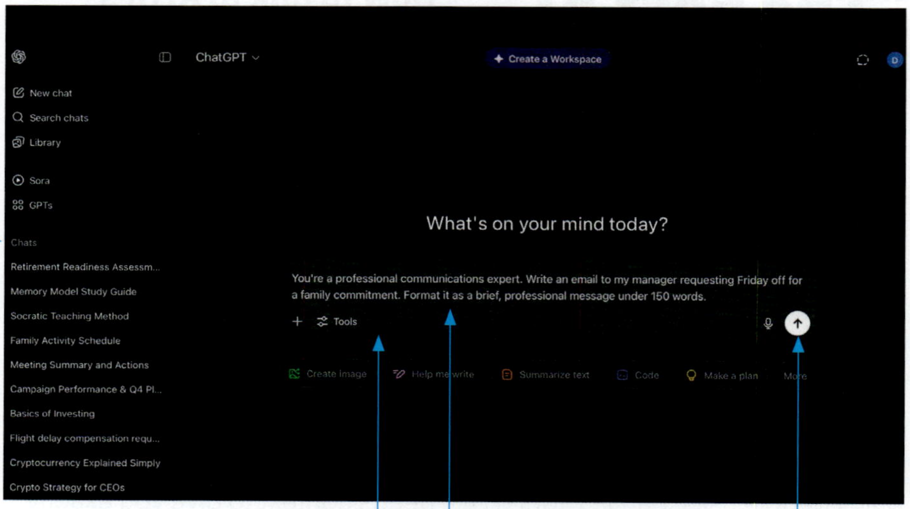

1 Text input box at bottom

2 **Send** button

3 Previous conversation history

4 Example of a well-structured prompt being typed

"Explain [mortgage refinancing] like I'm interviewing for a job and need to sound informed but not expert."

"Help me write a polite but firm email about [repeated noise complaints] to [my upstairs neighbor]."

"Give me five creative solutions for [organizing a home office in a studio apartment]."

The more specific details you provide, the more helpful the response. Don't worry about perfect grammar or formal language—write like you're explaining the situation to a friend. The AI will understand conversational English better than stiff, formal requests—and will ignore spelling mistakes and typos.

Remember that you can always refine the output. If the first response isn't quite right, don't give up; just tell the AI what to change: "Make it shorter", "Use simpler language", or "Add more specific examples". Think of it as a collaboration, not a one-shot deal.

Quick Start

Copy this exact prompt: "I'm planning a dinner party for 6 people, including one vegetarian and one person who can't eat gluten. Suggest a complete menu with one main dish that works for everyone."

Sometimes, it helps to explain the problem you're looking at and ask the AI what clarifying questions it might have, before telling it what output you want.

When AI gets creative

Beyond basic writing tasks, generative AI shines as a creative collaborator across countless projects. This is where AI moves from being a really helpful creative tool to becoming a genuine creative partner.

The key shift happens when you stop thinking of AI as a question-and-answer service and start treating it as a brainstorming buddy who never runs out of ideas. Whether you're planning events, solving problems, or learning new skills, AI brings fresh perspectives and systematic approaches to creative challenges.

Content creation and communication

For content creation, it transforms rough ideas into polished pieces. Draft online content like blog posts by providing key points and letting AI develop them into flowing prose. Generate social media captions that match your brand voice by sharing a few examples of posts you like. Create newsletter content by outlining topics and having AI write engaging introductions and transitions.

Communication becomes more effective when you have a writing partner who never judges your first drafts. Craft difficult conversations by describing the relationship dynamics and desired outcomes. Write complaint letters that get results by explaining your frustration and the resolution you're seeking. Develop presentation outlines that engage your specific audience by describing who they are and what they care about.

Problem-solving and planning

Problem-solving becomes more systematic with AI assistance. Tackle business challenges by describing your situation and constraints, then ask for multiple solution approaches. Organize your household by getting customized systems based on your family size, schedules, and living space. Plan travel itineraries that balance must-see attractions

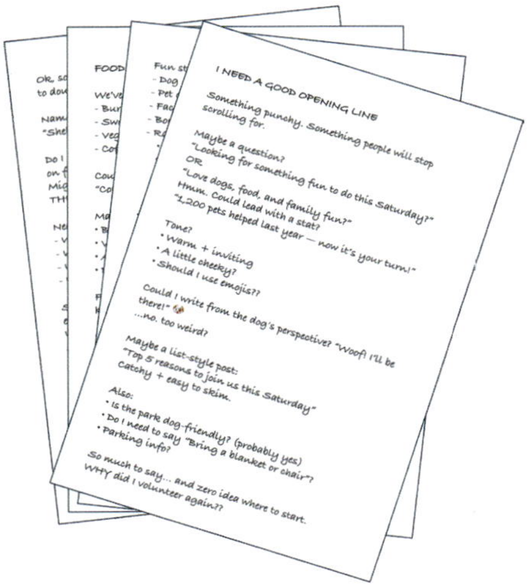

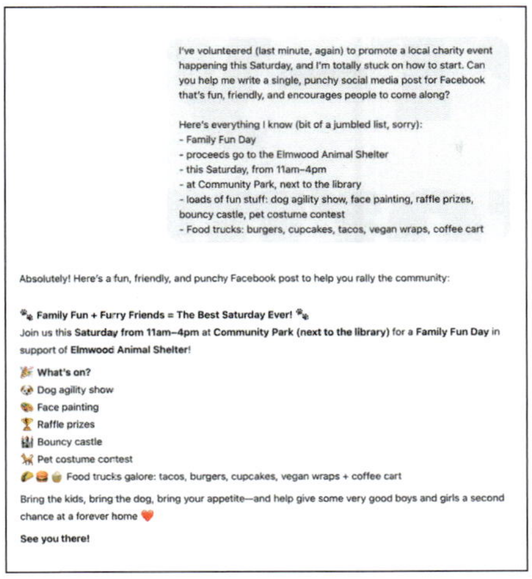

I've volunteered (last minute, again) to promote a local charity event happening this Saturday, and I'm totally stuck on how to start. Can you help me write a single, punchy social media post for Facebook that's fun, friendly, and encourages people to come along?

Here's everything I know (bit of a jumbled list, sorry):
- Family Fun Day
- proceeds go to the Elmwood Animal Shelter
- this Saturday, from 11am–4pm
- at Community Park, next to the library
- loads of fun stuff: dog agility show, face painting, raffle prizes, bouncy castle, pet costume contest
- Food trucks: burgers, cupcakes, tacos, vegan wraps, coffee cart

Absolutely! Here's a fun, friendly, and punchy Facebook post to help you rally the community:

🐾 **Family Fun + Furry Friends = The Best Saturday Ever!** 🐾
Join us this **Saturday from 11am–4pm** at **Community Park (next to the library)** for a **Family Fun Day** in support of **Elmwood Animal Shelter**!

🎉 **What's on?**
🐶 Dog agility show
🎨 Face painting
🏆 Raffle prizes
🏰 Bouncy castle
🐕 Pet costume contest
🌮🍔🧁 Food trucks galore: tacos, burgers, cupcakes, vegan wraps + coffee cart

Bring the kids, bring the dog, bring your appetite—and help give some very good boys and girls a second chance at a forever home ❤️

See you there!

with your specific interests and energy levels.

Project management gets supercharged when you have an assistant that considers every angle. Break down complex goals into manageable steps with realistic timelines. Create contingency plans for common obstacles. Develop decision-making frameworks that account for your specific priorities and constraints.

Learning and personal projects

Learning and teaching get supercharged when you have an infinitely patient tutor. Generate study guides that match your learning style. Create lesson plans that engage different types of learners. Get complex topics explained using analogies from your hobbies or profession—suddenly, quantum computing makes sense when explained through cooking metaphors.

Personal projects benefit from AI's endless patience for details. Plan parties with customized themes, decorations, and menu ideas based on your budget and guest preferences. Get gift ideas that match the recipient's interests, relationship, and your price range. Receive hobby guidance that starts at your current skill level and provides a clear progression path.

Fitness and wellness planning becomes personalized when you describe your specific situation, limitations, and goals. Create workout routines that work with your schedule and available equipment. Develop meal plans that accommodate your dietary preferences, cooking skills, and family needs.

"AI excels at taking your rough ideas and helping you develop them into polished results."

Hot Tip

AI can help you learn new skills by creating personalized curricula based on your current knowledge and available time.

Your next steps

This week, try one of the three sample prompts from this article with ChatGPT, Claude, or Perplexity. Pick whichever situation most closely matches something you're dealing with right now. Don't overthink it—just describe your situation in plain English and see what happens.

This month, identify one recurring task where AI could save you significant time. Maybe it's writing weekly team updates, creating social media content, or explaining homework concepts to your kids. Use AI consistently for this one task until it becomes second nature.

Going forward, experiment with different AI tools for the same task. You'll quickly discover which tool's style matches your needs for different situations. Some people love ChatGPT's conversational approach for brainstorming but prefer Claude's precisional approach for important documents.

Going deeper

The following articles will dive deeper into each major AI tool, showing you exactly how to set up accounts, navigate interfaces, and master the prompts that get you the best results. You'll move from basic questions to advanced techniques that unlock each tool's full potential.

You already know how to have conversations—now, you just have more interesting conversation partners. The same skills that help you explain problems to friends or colleagues will help you get incredible results from AI. The only difference? These conversation partners never get tired, never judge your questions, and always have time to help. ■

ChatGPT—your brainstorming buddy who never sleeps

You've heard about ChatGPT from that friend who won't stop talking about how it wrote their wedding toast, or from headlines about students using it for homework. But ChatGPT isn't just for tech wizards or cheaters. It's your personal brainstorming buddy who never sleeps, never judges your 5 AM shower thoughts, and enjoys helping you untangle that complaint email you've been putting off for weeks.

In the next 20 minutes, you'll go from ChatGPT curious to ChatGPT capable. You'll have your free account set up, know exactly which buttons do what, and—here's the best part—you'll walk away with three completed projects: a personalized weekend getaway plan, a crystal-clear explanation of something complex (perfect for impressing at dinner parties), and that perfectly worded complaint email that actually gets results.

What ChatGPT really is

Think of ChatGPT as the world's most patient conversation partner—one who's read millions of books, articles, and websites, and genuinely wants to help you think through problems.

Beyond Google and Wikipedia

Here's what throws people off: ChatGPT isn't Google. While Google finds existing web pages, ChatGPT creates fresh responses tailored to your exact question. Ask Google about Italian restaurants, and you'll get a list of websites. Ask ChatGPT, and it'll consider your dietary restrictions, budget, and whether you're dining with toddlers or trying to impress a date.

It's also not Wikipedia spitting facts at you. ChatGPT will tell you when it's unsure about something or when information might be outdated. Its knowledge has a cutoff date, so it won't know who won last night's game or today's stock prices.

Warning

ChatGPT's knowledge stops at its training cutoff—always verify recent events, current prices, or breaking news with up-to-date sources.

What makes it different?

What ChatGPT excels at is being your thinking partner—helping you explore ideas, solve problems, and find new angles you hadn't considered. Unlike search engines that assume you know what you're looking for, ChatGPT helps you figure out what questions to ask in the first place.

The magic happens in the conversation. You can ask follow-up questions, request changes, or dive deeper into any response. It remembers what you've talked about in that chat, building on previous messages to help you develop ideas. Think of it as having a knowledgeable

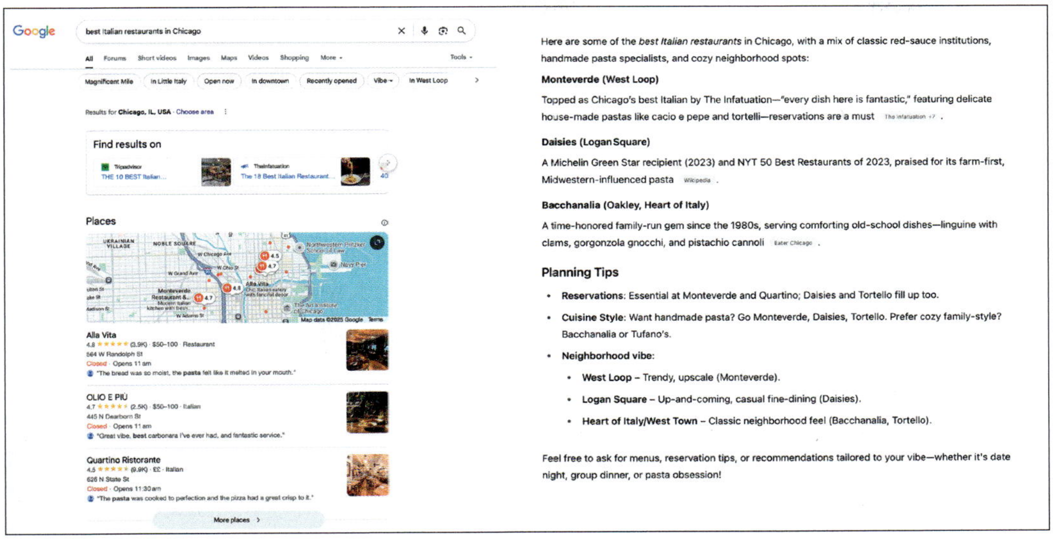

Hot Tip
Use a personal email, not work—some companies block AI tools, and you want 24/7 access to your brainstorming buddy.

friend who's always available and endlessly patient with your questions.

Did You Know?
ChatGPT can maintain context for thousands of words in a single conversation, remembering details from your first message even after dozens of exchanges.

Common misconceptions cleared up

ChatGPT doesn't "think" like humans do—it predicts what words should come next based on patterns it learned during training. This makes it excellent at language tasks but terrible at math beyond basic calculations. It can't browse the internet in real time or remember conversations from yesterday.

Most importantly, ChatGPT isn't trying to replace your judgment. It's a tool for enhancing your thinking, not doing your thinking for you. You bring the context, goals, and final decisions. ChatGPT brings perspective, suggestions, and infinite patience with your "what if" scenarios.

Now that you know what you're working with, let's get you set up in under 5 minutes.

Zero to ChatGPT hero in 5 minutes

Getting started with ChatGPT is easier than setting up a new TV remote—and infinitely more useful.

Creating your account

First, open your web browser and navigate to **chat.openai.com**. You'll see a clean, simple homepage with two buttons: **Log in** and **Sign up**. Here's where people often slip up—you want **Sign up**, not **Log in**, even though the **Log in** button might look more prominent.

Click "Sign up" and you'll see three options: continue with Google, continue with Microsoft, or use your email. Any option works fine, but I recommend using a personal email rather than your work address.

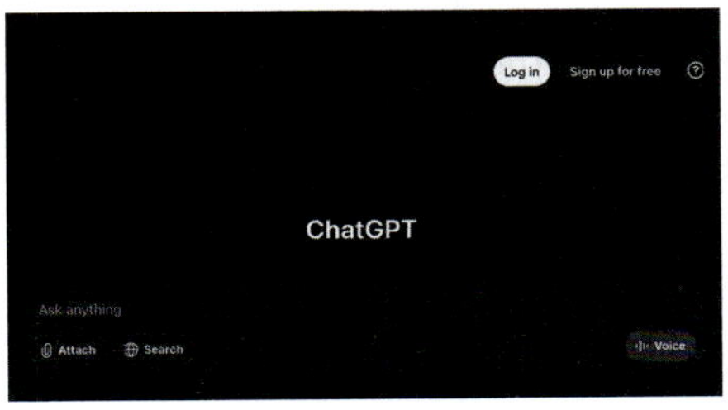

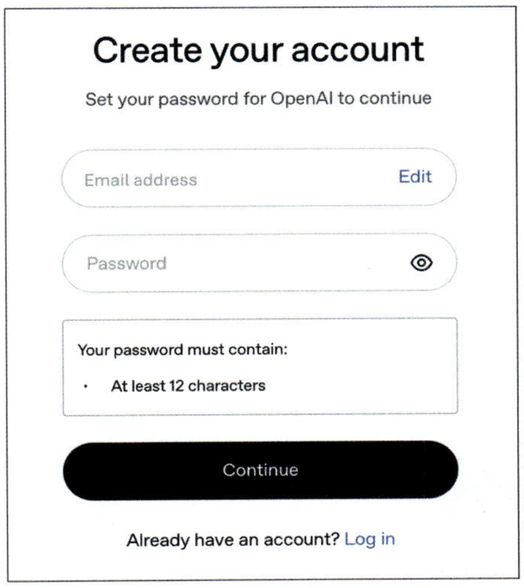

If you choose email, follow these numbered steps:

1. Enter your email address in the top field
2. Create a secure password (ChatGPT will use this for all future logins)
3. Click **Continue**

Verification and first login

ChatGPT will send a verification email within seconds. Check your Inbox and Spam folders if needed. The email will have the subject line **Verify your email address** from OpenAI.

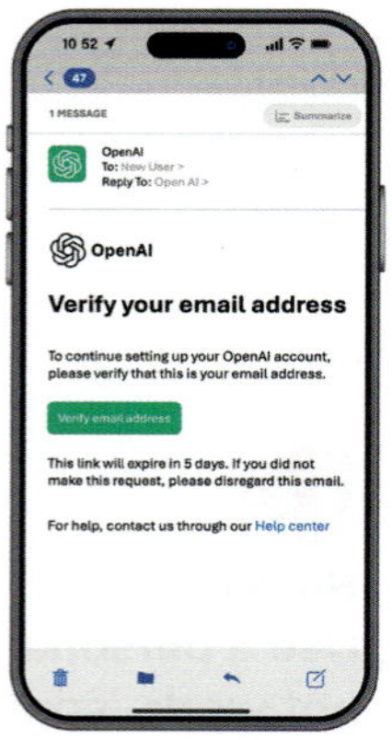

Click the verification link in the email. This will redirect you back to ChatGPT, where you'll complete a quick "I'm not a robot" puzzle. These usually involve clicking on traffic lights or bicycles—standard internet security stuff.

Once verified, you're in! The first time you log in, ChatGPT might show you a few welcome screens explaining basic features. You can click through these quickly—we'll cover everything important in much more detail.

Quick Start
Skip the welcome tour—everything you need to know is right here in this article.

That's it. From "I don't have an account" to "I'm chatting with AI" in under five minutes. No credit card required, no complex setup process, no technical knowledge needed. Just you and your new AI assistant, ready to tackle whatever's on your mind.

Your ChatGPT command center

The ChatGPT interface looks deceptively simple—like a text message app. But knowing these six areas will multiply your results by 10:

The main interface elements

1. **The conversation area** sits front and center. This is where your messages and ChatGPT's responses appear. Your messages show up on the right in darker text, while ChatGPT's responses appear on the left in a lighter shade. Just like texting, except your conversation partner has read most of the internet.

2. **The New chat button** lives in the top-left corner. This is your fresh start button. Each new chat begins with a clean slate—ChatGPT won't remember previous conversations. Use this when switching topics completely or when you want to approach something from a new angle.

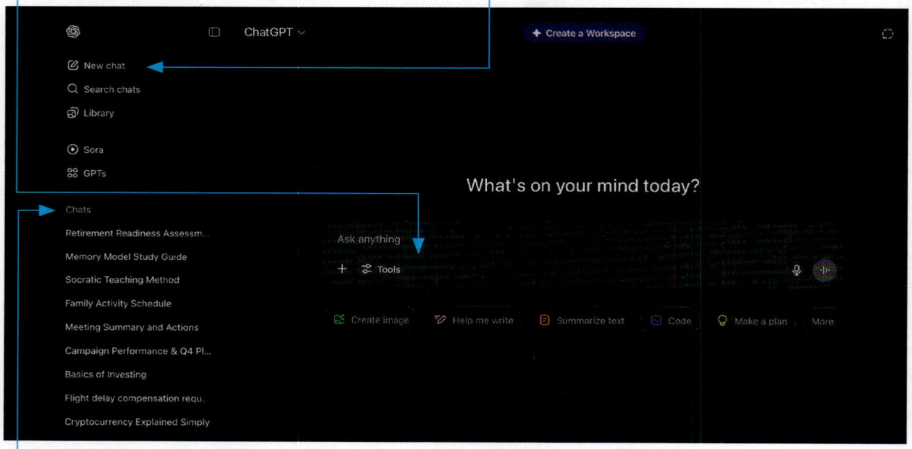

3. **Chat history** runs down the left sidebar. Every conversation gets saved automatically with a title based on your first message.

You can return to any previous chat, rename them for easy finding, or delete ones you no longer need. Think of it as your idea archive.

Hidden power features

Here's where most people miss the magic. Hover over any of ChatGPT's responses and you'll see small icons appear:

1. **Copy button** grabs the entire response for pasting elsewhere
2. **Thumbs up/down** helps train the system (and helps other users)
3. **Regenerate button** (curved arrow) is your do-over option when you want ChatGPT to try again with a different approach

You can also edit your own messages after sending them. Made a typo? Want to add more detail? Click the pencil icon next to your message, make changes, and ChatGPT will give a fresh response to your edited version. The original response stays visible but grayed out, so you can compare different approaches.

Did You Know?
Editing a message creates an alternate conversation branch—you can explore multiple approaches to the same problem without losing your original results.

Organization that actually works

Here's a power move most people miss: starting fresh chats for different projects. Your "Weekend Trip Planning" chat stays separate from "Work Email Help", keeping each conversation focused and easy to revisit. ChatGPT performs better when it's not juggling multiple unrelated topics.

The input box stretches across the bottom. Hit **Enter** to send, or **Shift** + **Enter** to add a line break. The paper airplane icon sends your message if you prefer clicking.

Next Level

Use Shift + Enter to write multi-paragraph prompts before sending—better organization leads to better responses.

Interface mastered. Now for the secret sauce: knowing how to ask for what you want.

The anatomy of a perfect prompt

The difference between "meh" and "mind-blowing" ChatGPT responses comes down to how you ask. You can find many prompt templates across the web, but I have found two that will cover most situations.

RTF: for everyday discussions

For most tasks, the RTF template gives you everything you need:

- **Role:** What perspective do you want? "You're a travel consultant..." or "As a nutrition expert..." Helps ChatGPT know which knowledge context to bring in.
- **Task:** What specific job needs doing? "Create an itinerary..." or "Explain the benefits of...".
- **Format:** How do you want the output? "Day-by-day schedule..." or "Simple bullet points...".

Let's see RTF in action with a work email:

Weak prompt: "Help me write an email asking for Friday off."

Strong RTF prompt: "You're a professional communications expert. Write an email to my manager requesting Friday off for a family commitment. Format it as a brief, professional message under 150 words."

RTF works perfectly for straightforward requests where you know exactly what you want.

SPARK: for complex projects

When you need more comprehensive results, the SPARK template covers more angles:

- **Situation:** Set the scene. Who are you? What's happening? Why does this matter?
- **Purpose:** What are you trying to achieve? What's your end goal?
- **Action:** What should ChatGPT do? Explain, create, analyze, compare, suggest.
- **Requirements:** Specific constraints, tone, length, things to include or avoid.
- **Knowledge:** Special context—ChatGPT needs to understand your situation.

Here's how you might approach a complex travel planning scenario:

Weak prompt: "Help me plan a 3-day trip to Rome, including activities for my teenage kids."

SPARK prompt: "I'm planning a 3-day trip to Rome with my two teenage kids (15 and 17) who get bored easily with traditional tourist stuff. I want to show them history while keeping them engaged, and create memories we'll all treasure. Create a detailed itinerary that blends must-see historical sites with activities teens actually enjoy.

You're a professional communications expert. Write an email to my manager requesting Friday off for a family commitment. Format it as a brief, professional message under 150 words.

Sure! Here's the email, as requested:

Subject: Request for Leave – This Friday

Hi [Manager's Name],

I hope you're well. I'd like to request this Friday off due to a family commitment. I'll ensure all my responsibilities are up to date beforehand and can provide a handover if needed.

Please let me know if this works or if you need anything from me in the lead-up.

Best regards,
[Your Name]

Help me write an email asking for Friday off

Sure! Here's the email, as requested:

Subject: Day Off Request

Hi [Manager's Name],

I wanted to ask if I could take this Friday off. Please let me know if that's okay or if you need anything from me before then.

Thanks,
[Your Name]

Help me plan a 3-day trip to Rome, including activities for my teenage kids

Sure! Here's a simple 3-day itinerary for your trip to Rome with teenage kids:

Day 1: Ancient Rome

- Morning: Visit the Colosseum (get skip-the-line tickets)
- Afternoon: Explore the Roman Forum and Palatine Hill
- Evening: Walk around the area near the Altare della Patria and grab dinner nearby

Day 2: Vatican City

- Morning: Tour the Vatican Museums and the Sistine Chapel
- Afternoon: Visit St. Peter's Basilica
- Evening: Relax at Piazza Navona and try some gelato

Day 3: City Highlights

- Morning: See the Pantheon and Trevi Fountain
- Afternoon: Visit the Spanish Steps and maybe do some shopping
- Evening: Have a pizza dinner in Trastevere

Let me know if you want hotel suggestions or more details!

Keep daily walking under 2 miles, include specific restaurant names, budget around $200 per day for activities, and we're staying near the Colosseum. My kids love food experiences, interactive activities, and Instagram-worthy spots, but hate long museum walks."

See the difference? SPARK gives ChatGPT rich context to create something truly personalized, while RTF handles everyday tasks efficiently.

Building your prompt library

Both templates adapt to any situation. Need something casual? Adjust the role and requirements. Want a different format? Change how you specify the output. ChatGPT responds instantly to your specifications.

Hot Tip

Save your best prompts in a notes app—build your own prompt library for instant results.

For example, here's a job interview preparation challenge using each template:

RTF approach: "You're a career coach. Help me practice answering 'What's your greatest weakness?'. Format as three different answer examples with brief explanations."

I'm planning a 3-day trip to Rome with my two teenage kids (15 and 17) who get bored easily with traditional tourist stuff. I want to show them history while keeping them engaged, and create memories we'll all treasure. Create a detailed itinerary that blends must-see historical sites with activities teens actually enjoy. Keep daily walking under 2 miles, include specific restaurant names, budget around $200 per day for activities, and we're staying near the Colosseum. My kids love food experiences, interactive activities, and Instagram-worthy spots, but hate long museum walks

Here's a polished 3-day Rome itinerary that balances iconic history with engaging, teen-friendly experiences—keeping walking light and fun high:

Day 1: Ancient Rome & Gladiator Vibes
Focus: Immersive history + action

- **Morning**:
  - *Gladiator School Experience* (Via Appia Antica): 2-hour hands-on class where you train like a Roman gladiator. Super interactive, fun for teens, and educational without being dry.
  - **Budget**: ~$80/person
- **Lunch**: *Taverna dei Quaranta* – rustic Roman fare just a short walk from your hotel
- **Afternoon**:
  - *Colosseum Express Tour* (60–90 mins): Small-group or self-guided using an app. Skip extended history lessons—just enough info for context and great photo ops.
  - Stroll briefly around the Roman Forum overlook (no full walk-through to keep it short)
- **Evening**:
  - Gelato crawl from *Gelateria La Romana* to *Frigidarium* (a 15-minute Uber ride covers the distance)
  - Sunset photos at *Piazza Venezia* (Altare della Patria – elevator to the top for panoramic views)
- **Total Walking**: ~1.5 miles

Day 2: Vatican Highlights & Food Fun
Focus: Quick culture + hands-on food

- **Morning**:
  - *Vatican Early Access Tour* (1.5-hour express version—focus on Sistine Chapel + highlights only)
  - **Budget**: ~$60/person
- **Lunch**: *Pizzarium Bonci* – famous for creative Roman pizza by the slice, loved by teens
- **Afternoon**:
  - *Tiramisu or Pasta-Making Class* (near Trastevere or Campo de' Fiori): Teens get to cook (and eat!) with a local chef. Hands-on and Instagram-worthy.
  - **Budget**: ~$50–70/person
- **Evening**:
  - Explore *Trastevere*: relaxed vibe, colorful streets, great street performers
  - Dinner at *Osteria Der Belli* – cozy, seafood-friendly, and teen-approved
- **Total Walking**: ~1.8 miles

Day 3: Insta-Worthy Rome & Hidden Gems
Focus: Visual impact + chill exploring

- **Morning**:
  - *Pantheon* + *Trevi Fountain* early to beat crowds
  - Stop at *Café Doria* near Piazza Venezia for a scenic cappuccino or smoothie
- **Lunch**: *Trapizzino Testaccio* – hybrid of pizza and sandwich, fun and trendy
- **Afternoon**:
  - *VR Experience Rome Reborn* (near Piazza Navona): 45-minute immersive headset tour of ancient Rome as it was—perfect for tech-loving teens
  - Quick photo stop at *Spanish Steps* and window-shop nearby
  - **Budget**: ~$25/person
- **Evening**:
  - *Dinner at Ristorante Aroma* (if budget allows, with Colosseum view – book in advance), or casual dinner at *La Carbonara* in Monti neighborhood
  - End with photos near the lit-up Colosseum at night
- **Total Walking**: ~1.7 miles

Let me know if you'd like Google Maps routes, reservation links, or to swap any activities!

Absolutely — here are **three strong example answers** to *"What's your greatest weakness?"*, each with a brief explanation of why it works:

1. The Classic-but-Managed Weakness

Answer:

> "I can be a bit of a perfectionist, which sometimes means I spend more time than necessary refining details. Over time, I've learned to balance high standards with efficiency by prioritizing what really matters and using tools like checklists and timeboxing to stay focused and on track."

Why it works:

- It's a common, relatable weakness.
- It shows self-awareness and a proactive approach to improvement.
- It reframes the trait as one with benefits (attention to detail).

2. The Skill Gap with Growth

Answer:

> "Early in my career, I struggled with public speaking. Presenting in front of groups made me nervous. I recognized it as a vital skill, so I joined Toastmasters and volunteered for small presentations. Now I lead team meetings and feel much more confident speaking up in front of others."

Why it works:

- Shows vulnerability without being disqualifying.
- Demonstrates a growth mindset and concrete action.
- Ends on a positive note with visible progress.

3. The Overused Strength Reframed

Answer:

> "I tend to take on too much responsibility when working in teams, because I want everything to go well. But I've learned that trusting others and delegating properly leads to better collaboration and results. I now focus on setting clear roles and checking in regularly rather than trying to do it all myself."

Why it works:

- Shows leadership potential and ownership.
- Acknowledges the risk of burnout or micromanaging.
- Highlights growth and team awareness.

Let me know if you'd like to tailor one of these to a specific role or industry!

SPARK approach: "I have a job interview next week for a marketing manager position at a tech startup. I'm worried about the "weakness" question because feedback from my last interview was that my answer to this question felt too rehearsed. I want to sound authentic while still presenting myself professionally. Help me develop and practice responses to "What's your greatest weakness?". Give me multiple approaches I can choose from, explain why each works, and help me sound genuine rather than scripted. I tend to be a perfectionist and sometimes take on too much, but I've been working on delegation and time management."

✅ **Approach 1: The Honest Self-Awareness Angle (Perfectionism + Growth)**

Tone: Reflective, humble, grounded.
Example Answer:

> "I've noticed that I sometimes fall into perfectionist habits — spending too much time tweaking campaigns or reworking presentations because I want everything to be just right. In a fast-moving environment, I realized that can slow things down or delay feedback. Lately, I've been focusing more on hitting key milestones and getting work into review stages earlier, which has helped me balance quality with speed. It's still a work in progress, but it's something I'm intentionally improving."

Why it works:

- Acknowledges the weakness without sounding dramatic.
- Shows clear self-awareness and evolution.
- Feels personal and unscripted — "still a work in progress" adds authenticity.

✅ **Approach 2: The Leadership Lens (Overcommitting + Delegation)**

Tone: Managerial, thoughtful, team-oriented.
Example Answer:

> "In previous roles, I've had a tendency to take on too much myself — especially when a deadline is tight or the stakes are high. I used to think the best way to ensure quality was to own as much as possible. But I've realized that can hold back the team and create bottlenecks. I've been deliberately working on delegation and trust — setting clearer ownership across the team and empowering others to lead parts of a campaign. It's actually made our projects stronger and helped me step more fully into a leadership role."

Why it works:

- Focuses on a real leadership challenge.
- Emphasizes a transition from individual contributor to true manager.
- Shows reflection and a shift in mindset — startup teams will appreciate that.

✅ **Approach 3: The Fast-Paced Environment Fit (Speed vs. Detail)**

Tone: Practical, results-oriented, startup-aligned.
Example Answer:

> "In the past, I've sometimes gotten too caught up in the details — like perfecting copy or obsessing over analytics dashboards — and that's not always compatible with startup pace. I've learned that in growth-stage environments, done is often better than perfect, and fast feedback loops matter more than polished execution. I've shifted toward building MVPs, testing early, and optimizing over time. That's been a big mindset shift for me, but it's really helped me move faster and drive results."

Why it works:

- Tailored to a tech startup context.
- Frames your perfectionism as something you're actively adapting.
- Demonstrates you understand the trade-offs in fast-paced work.

🔁 **How to Make Any of These Sound More Natural**

To avoid sounding rehearsed:

- **Pause slightly** before answering to show you're reflecting.
- **Use conversational language** (e.g., "I've noticed," "I used to think...").
- **Include small, specific examples** (e.g., "There was a campaign last quarter where...").
- **End with progress**, not perfection — this keeps it relatable.

Both work—RTF for quick answers; SPARK for comprehensive solutions.

Power follow-ups

One more power technique: the follow-up. Your first prompt starts the conversation, but don't stop there. Ask ChatGPT to:

- "Make it more formal."
- "Add specific examples."
- "Explain that part in more detail."
- "Give me three alternatives."
- "Now make it funny."

Each follow-up refines the response, getting you closer to exactly what you need. ChatGPT remembers the entire conversation, so you don't have to repeat yourself.

Formula learned? Time to put it to work on your first project.

Hot Tip

If you find you are using the same kind of prompt repeatedly, then you might consider creating a custom GPT—a topic we'll cover in a future issue.

Project 1: weekend city break planner

Ready to put everything together? These three projects will give you hands-on experience with different types of ChatGPT conversations.

Let's plan your perfect weekend getaway using the SPARK framework for a comprehensive approach.

Step 1: Copy this SPARK prompt, filling in your details:

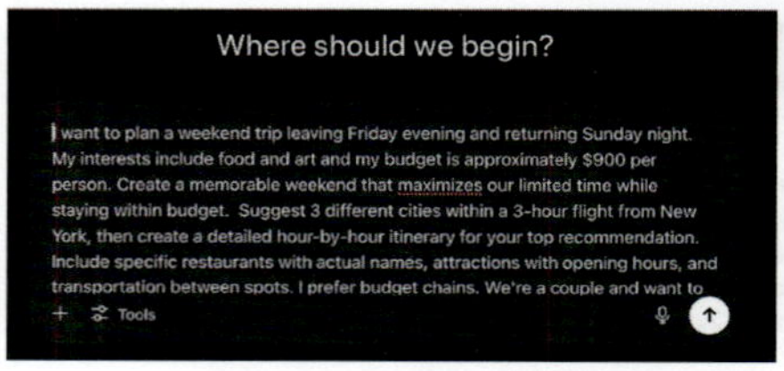

- I want to plan a weekend trip leaving Friday evening and returning Sunday night. My interests include [pick 2: food/music/art/outdoors/history/shopping] and my budget is approximately $[X] per person.
- Create a memorable weekend that maximizes our limited time while staying within budget.
- Suggest 3 different cities within a 3-hour flight from [your city], then create a detailed hour-by-hour itinerary for your top recommendation.
- Include restaurants with actual names, attractions with opening hours, and transportation between spots. I prefer [pick one: luxury stays/boutique hotels/Airbnb/budget chains].
- We're [solo/couple/family with kids ages X] and want to balance planned activities with spontaneous exploration.

Step 2: Review ChatGPT's response. You'll get three city suggestions with reasoning, plus a detailed itinerary for the top choice.

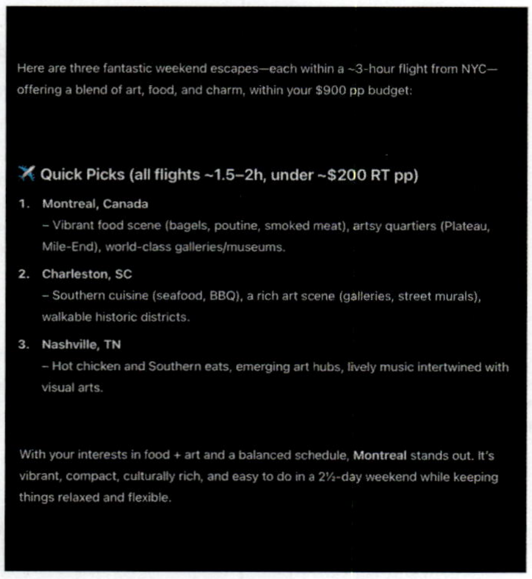

Step 3: Customize further with these follow-ups:

- "Tell me more about that Saturday food tour."
- "What's the weather typically like that time of year?"
- "Give me backup restaurant options in case the first choices are booked."
- "Add estimated costs for each activity."

Variations for different travel styles

- **Romance focus:** Add "traveling with partner, looking for romantic spots, prefer intimate dining."
- **Family version:** Include "with kids ages X and Y, need kid-friendly activities and restaurants."
- **Solo adventure:** Specify "solo traveler, want to meet people, interested in local culture."

Quick Start

Screenshot or copy the final itinerary into your notes app—ChatGPT conversations can be hard to find later when you're actually traveling.

Look at what ChatGPT delivers: not just city suggestions, but reasoning for each choice based on your interests. For the top pick, you get restaurant names with cuisine types, attraction details with hours, and even notes about transportation options. This isn't generic travel guide stuff—it's personalized to your preferences and constraints.

Within minutes, you've got a weekend plan that would take hours to research manually. And unlike generic travel websites, this one's built around your specific interests, budget, and travel style.

Project 2: the "explain like I'm 10" generator

We'll use RTF for this straightforward explanatory task.

Step 1: Use this RTF template:

- You're an expert teacher who makes complex topics fun and understandable.
- Explain [complex topic] to a curious 10-year-old using analogies they'd understand and include one "wow" fact that would impress their friends.
- Keep it under 200 words and make sure a real 10-year-old would say "cool!", not "huh?".

Step 2: Let's try it with cryptocurrency:

Notice how ChatGPT transforms a complex financial concept into something tangible. Trading cards, classroom rules, keeping track in notebooks—all concepts a 10-year-old already understands. The "wow" fact about pizza purchases makes it real and memorable.

Step 3: Here's where it gets interesting. Take that same topic and try a different RTF approach:

- You're a business consultant explaining technology to executives.
- Explain cryptocurrency's strategic implications for a CEO who needs to make decisions about it.
- Professional brief focusing on business opportunities and risks, 300 words maximum.

Same topic, completely different approach. ChatGPT adapts its language, examples, and focus based on the audience and communication preferences.

More topics to try

Try these topics with the 10-year-old prompt:

- How does my phone know where I am?
- Why do we dream?
- What makes airplanes stay up?
- How does the internet actually work?
- Why can't we just print more money?

Did You Know?

If you can explain something to a 10-year-old, you truly understand it—and you'll remember it far longer than memorizing technical definitions.

The power move? Once you understand something at the 10-year-old level, you truly get it.

Sure! Let's say you and your classmates trade special trading cards at school. Instead of using real money, you make up your own class currency—let's call it **CardCoin**.

Now, there's no teacher or bank in charge. Instead, **every kid has a notebook** to track every trade that happens. If Maya gives Jack 3 CardCoins for a shiny dragon card, **everyone writes it down** in their notebook. That way, no one can lie or cheat—because if your notebook doesn't match everyone else's, it's obvious you're fibbing!

That's how **cryptocurrency** works. It's like digital trading cards, and the notebooks are like **the blockchain** —a record that everyone shares to keep things fair.

And here's the coolest part: The first real thing someone ever bought with a cryptocurrency (called **Bitcoin**) was **two pizzas**. Today, those pizzas would be worth over **$600 million**. That's the most expensive pizza in history! 🍕 💰

Pretty wild, right?

You can explain it to anyone, and you'll remember it far longer than memorizing technical definitions.

Project 3: the complaint email that gets results

That airline lost your luggage? Restaurant served cold food? Let's channel your frustration into an email that gets action, not excuses.

Step 1: Your RTF power prompt:

- You're a professional business communicator skilled at resolving conflicts.
- Write a complaint email about [specific issue]. The situation: [what happened, when, where]. What I want: [refund/replacement/apology].
- Firm but professional tone under 250 words with clear request and timeline. Include specific details that show I'm reasonable but experienced with customer service.

Step 2: Real example:

"You're a professional business communicator skilled at resolving conflicts. Help me write a complaint email about a delayed flight. The situation: Flight AA1234 from Dallas to Miami on January 15 was delayed 4 hours due to "crew scheduling", causing me to miss an important client meeting. What I want: Compensation per

Cryptocurrency: Strategic Summary for CEOs

Cryptocurrency offers both opportunity and risk for modern businesses.

Opportunities:

- **Revenue & Reach:** Accepting crypto can reduce fees and attract global, tech-savvy customers.
- **Innovation:** Tokenization and decentralized finance (DeFi) enable new funding models and asset liquidity.
- **Brand Advantage:** Early adoption signals innovation and leadership in digital transformation.

Risks:

- **Regulation:** Legal uncertainty can impact operations and compliance.
- **Volatility:** Crypto values fluctuate widely, posing financial risk.
- **Security:** Custody and cyber threats require robust safeguards.
- **Reputation:** Misaligned crypto use can damage brand trust.

Recommendation: Treat crypto as a strategic tool, not just a financial asset. Begin with controlled pilots, align with business goals, and build internal capabilities.

Subject: Request for Compensation for Flight AA1234 Delay on January 15

Dear American Airlines Customer Relations,

I'm writing regarding Flight AA1234 from Dallas to Miami on January 15, which was delayed over four hours due to crew scheduling. As a result, I missed a critical client meeting that had been confirmed weeks in advance, impacting both my business and reputation.

I understand that delays happen, and I plan accordingly when disruptions are due to weather or other uncontrollable factors. However, this delay was within the airline's control. According to U.S. Department of Transportation guidelines, passengers are entitled to compensation in such cases.

I value reliability and chose American Airlines expecting professional service. Unfortunately, this experience fell short. I'm requesting compensation in accordance with DOT regulations. A travel credit, refund, or other fair resolution would be appropriate.

Please respond within 10 business days so we can resolve this efficiently.

Sincerely,
[Your Full Name]
[Your Contact Info]
[Ticket/Confirmation Number]

DOT guidelines. Tone: firm but professional—I want results, not to vent. Include specific details that show I'm a reasonable person facing an unreasonable situation. Keep it under 250 words and end with a clear request and timeline."

Step 3: Customize the tone with follow-ups:

- "Make it 20% firmer."
- "Add more emotional impact about the missed meeting."
- "Include that this is my third delay this month."
- "Make it shorter and more direct."

What makes these emails work?

See how ChatGPT structures this? Facts first, personal impact second, specific request third. No emotional rambling, no threats, just clear communication that respects everyone's time while firmly stating your position.
The email includes:

- Specific flight details (shows you're organized).
- Business impact (demonstrates real consequences).
- Reference to DOT guidelines (shows you know your rights).
- Reasonable timeline (14 days).
- Professional closing (maintains relationship).

Pro variations

- **Product issues:** Include order numbers, purchase dates, previous contact attempts.
- **Service complaints:** Mention specific employee names (positively when possible), time stamps, location details.
- **Subscription problems:** Reference account numbers, billing dates, previous loyalty.

Warning
Always proofread before sending—ChatGPT is excellent, but you know the full situation better than anyone.

The goal isn't to win a writing contest—it's to get your problem solved. These emails do exactly that by being clear, reasonable, and action-oriented.

Troubleshooting common issues

Even with the RTF and SPARK prompt templates, you'll occasionally hit snags. Here's how to identify problems, avoid common pitfalls, and get back on track quickly.

Prompts that sabotage your results

The Vague Ask: "Make this better" without explaining what "better" means. ChatGPT can't read your mind about whether you want something shorter, more formal, more detailed, or completely rewritten. Fix it by being specific: "Make this more professional" or "Shorten this to 100 words".

The Kitchen Sink: Cramming four different requests into one prompt. "Help me plan dinner, write a thank-you note, explain quantum physics, and suggest a workout routine." ChatGPT will try, but you'll get mediocre results for everything. Break complex requests into separate chats or use clear numbered sections.

The Assumption: Asking about "the meeting tomorrow" without explaining which meeting. ChatGPT doesn't know your calendar, your colleagues, or what you discussed yesterday. Always provide context, even if it feels obvious to you.

The Weak Framework: Using vague prompts like "help me with this" without applying a template like RTF or SPARK. These exist for a reason—use them to give ChatGPT the context it needs for excellent results.

Warning
ChatGPT has no memory between separate chats and no access to your personal information—provide context every time.

The Perfectionist Trap: Spending 20 minutes crafting the "perfect" first prompt instead of starting with something good and iterating. ChatGPT conversations are meant to be iterative—get something decent, then refine it. Don't let perfection be the enemy of good enough!

When ChatGPT misunderstands

The Wrong Direction: If you see ChatGPT going off in a completely wrong direction, don't start over. Type "Stop. I meant..." and clarify your actual request. ChatGPT will course-correct immediately.

The Generic Response: When responses are too generic or unhelpful, add more specific constraints. Instead of "Make it better" try "Make it more conversational" or "Add specific examples" or "Focus on the financial aspects".

Getting unstuck

When you're not sure what to ask: Start with "Help me think through..." and describe your situation. ChatGPT excels at helping you identify the right questions.

When responses are too long: Add "Keep responses under [X] words" to any prompt.

When responses are too short: Ask "Expand on that" or "Give me more detail about [specific part]".

Hot Tip
The Regenerate button often produces a completely different approach—use it when the first response is close but not quite what you are looking for.

Smart chat management

Start a new chat when:

- Switching to a completely different topic.
- The current chat has become cluttered with multiple subjects.
- You want to test different approaches.
- ChatGPT seems confused about what you're asking.

Continue the same chat when:

- Building on previous responses.
- Refining something you're working on.
- Asking follow-up questions.
- You want ChatGPT to remember earlier context.

Beyond the basics: what's next

You've mastered the fundamentals, completed real projects, and learned to troubleshoot issues. Now, let's explore advanced techniques and daily integration strategies that will make you a ChatGPT power user.

Advanced conversations

The real power of ChatGPT emerges when you treat it as a conversation, not a search engine. Each response becomes a stepping stone to deeper insights.

Try this progression:

1. Start with a broad question: "Explain the basics of investing."
2. Narrow down: "Focus on index funds for beginners."
3. Get specific: "Compare Vanguard and Fidelity index funds."
4. Make it personal: "Which would work better for someone saving $500 monthly?"

Each step builds on the previous response, creating a customized learning experience. Although you might have achieved a similar result with a SPARK-type template, sometimes it's OK to get there in steps, and then learn to prompt better next time.

The devil's advocate

Here's a technique that reveals blind spots in any decision: ask ChatGPT to present both sides of an argument.

"Present the strongest arguments for and against buying a house right now, then tell me which argument you find more compelling and why."

This works brilliantly for career decisions, investment choices, major purchases, business strategy, and even personal relationships. ChatGPT will present genuinely strong arguments for each position, then synthesize them into balanced advice.

Daily ideas

Start using ChatGPT for these everyday tasks:

- **Morning planning:** "Help me prioritize today's tasks based on deadlines and energy levels."
- **Email responses:** "Rewrite this email to sound more professional but still friendly."
- **Gift ideas:** "Suggest birthday gifts for a 12-year-old who loves art and science."
- **Cooking:** "What can I make with chicken, rice, peas and carrots?"

Tomorrow morning, open ChatGPT with your coffee! ■

Claude–the AI that actually reads the fine print

You're staring at a 47-page employee handbook, wondering if you're allowed to work from home on Fridays. Or maybe it's your mortgage documents, and you need to know about prepayment penalties. Claude thrives on exactly these moments–when you need an AI that actually enjoys reading the boring stuff.

While other AI tools excel at quick answers and creative brainstorming, Claude's superpower is digesting long, complex documents and making them human-friendly. Think of it as having a patient, detail-oriented assistant who never gets tired of explaining things.

What makes Claude different?

Claude stands apart in the AI landscape as the thoughtful, detail-oriented member of the family. While ChatGPT brainstorms and Perplexity researches, Claude excels at careful analysis and long-form work. It's the AI you turn to when accuracy and nuance matter more than speed.

Hot Tip

Claude works best when you give context about your audience—"Explain this like I'm a new employee" gets better results than just "Summarize this".

The Anthropic advantage

Built by Anthropic with a focus on helpfulness, harmlessness, and honesty, Claude takes a different approach to AI assistance. In practice, this means Claude will tell you when it's uncertain about something rather than confidently delivering wrong information. It's designed to be helpful without being pushy, and honest about its limitations.

This design philosophy shows up in everyday use. Claude won't just tell you what you want to hear—it will point out potential problems, suggest alternative interpretations, and help you think through implications you might have missed.

Warning

Always verify important details in legal or financial documents—Claude is excellent for understanding, but you still need professional advice for major decisions.

Reading comprehension that actually works

Claude can handle documents up to 200,000 words—equivalent to a 400-page book. Upload your contract, policy manual, or research paper, and Claude will read every word with the same attention to detail as a skilled human analyst. Unlike tools that skim for keywords, Claude understands context, catches subtle distinctions, and spots the details that matter.

This isn't just about length. Claude maintains comprehension across the entire document, connecting ideas from page 3 to conclusions on page 300. It remembers what it read at the beginning while processing the end, creating summaries that capture the full picture rather than just recent highlights.

Constitutional AI in action

What sets Claude apart is its Constitutional AI training—a system that makes it naturally cautious about giving advice that could cause harm. When reviewing your lease agreement, Claude won't just explain the terms; it will flag clauses that might be problematic and suggest questions to ask your landlord or lawyer.

This approach extends to financial documents, where Claude will highlight potential risks and suggest areas where you might want professional guidance. It's like having a careful friend who always reads the fine print and asks the right questions.

Getting started with Claude

Getting started with Claude is smoother than organizing your desk drawer—and dramatically more useful for tackling the paperwork that's been haunting your to-do list.

Setting up your Claude account

Navigate to **claude.ai** in your web browser. You'll land on a clean homepage that immediately communicates Claude's focus—this isn't about flashy features; it's about getting serious work done. Look for the **Sign Up** button in the top-right corner.

Click **Sign Up** and you'll see three straightforward options: continue with Google, continue with your email, or continue with your phone number. Unlike some AI platforms, Claude keeps the signup process refreshingly simple.

Hot Tip

Use your personal email rather than work—you want unrestricted access to your document-processing powerhouse.

If you choose email signup, here's your step-by-step process:

1. Enter your email address in the primary field
2. Create a secure password (you'll use this for all future sessions)

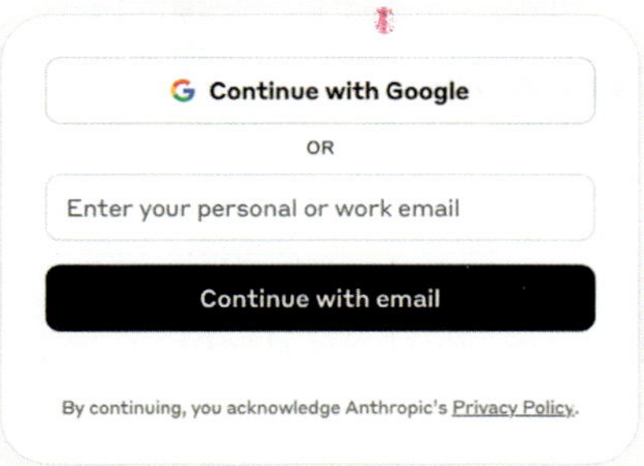

3. Confirm you're not a robot with the verification checkbox
4. Click **Create Account**

Account verification and welcome

Claude will immediately send a verification email—usually within 30 seconds. Check both your Inbox and Spam folders for an email from Anthropic with the subject "Verify your email address for Claude".

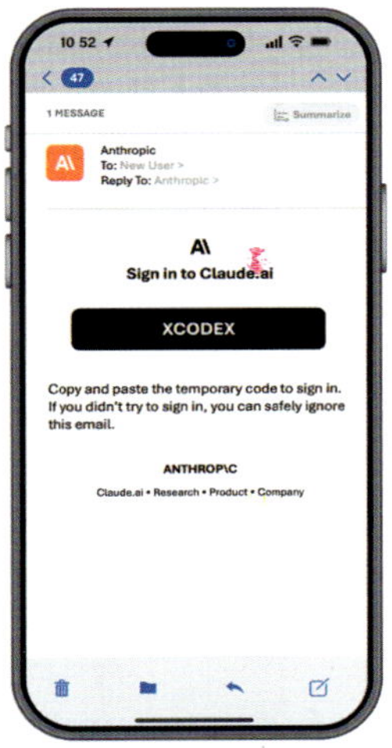

Click the verification link and you'll be redirected back to Claude's interface. Unlike other AI tools that bombard you with feature tours and upgrade prompts, Claude drops you straight into a clean workspace. You might see a brief welcome message, but there's no lengthy onboarding—Claude

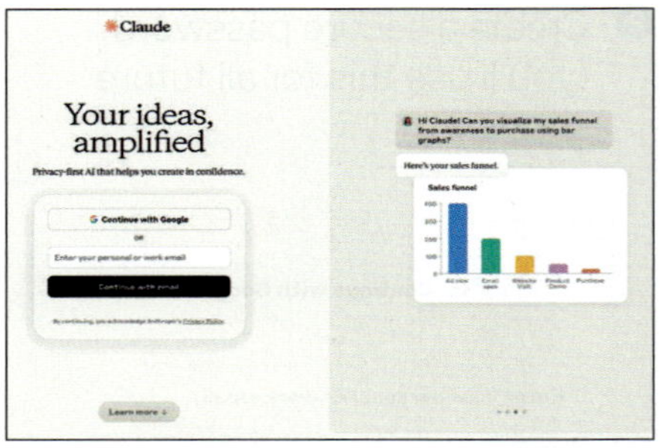

assumes you have documents to process and gets out of your way.

That's it. From "I need help with documents" to "I'm uploading my first contract" in under five minutes. No credit card required, no feature limitations that matter for document work, no technical setup. Just you and an AI that's genuinely excited to read whatever you've been avoiding.

Quick Start
Have a document ready? Skip ahead and upload it immediately—Claude learns your preferences faster through real work than through tutorials.

Mastering Claude's interface

Claude's interface looks almost too simple—like a notepad with superpowers. But understanding these key areas will transform how efficiently you process complex documents.

Core interface components

1. **The Conversation Canvas** dominates the center screen. This is where your document discussions unfold. Your messages appear in a clean, readable format, while Claude's responses flow naturally below. Unlike cluttered AI interfaces, Claude prioritizes readability—crucial when you're working through dense legal or technical content.

2. **The Upload Zone** sits prominently at the bottom of the interface. This drag-and-drop area accepts files up to 25MB, including PDFs, Word documents, Excel spreadsheets, images, and plain text files. When you drag a document over this area, it highlights clearly, and processing begins immediately upon drop.

3. **The Message Input Area** spans the bottom of the screen. Type your questions here, paste document text directly, or combine uploaded files with specific instructions. Hit **Enter** to send or **Shift** + **Enter** to add line breaks for longer, more detailed prompts.

Did You Know?
Claude can process multiple file formats simultaneously—upload your contract AND the related correspondence for comprehensive analysis.

Essential power features

4. **Conversation History** runs down the left sidebar, but Claude takes a different approach than other AI tools. Each conversation is automatically titled based on your documents and questions, making it easy to return to "Lease Agreement Analysis" or "Q3 Budget Review" weeks later.

5. **Response Actions** appear when you hover over Claude's messages. The **Copy** button grabs entire responses for pasting into emails or reports. The **Regenerate** option (circular arrow) gives you a completely fresh take on the same question—invaluable when analyzing complex documents from different angles.

6. **Message Editing** works differently in Claude. Click the **Edit** button next to your messages to refine your questions without losing context. This is particularly powerful for document analysis—start broad, then edit your message to focus on specific sections or concerns.

Document-processing indicators

Claude provides clear visual

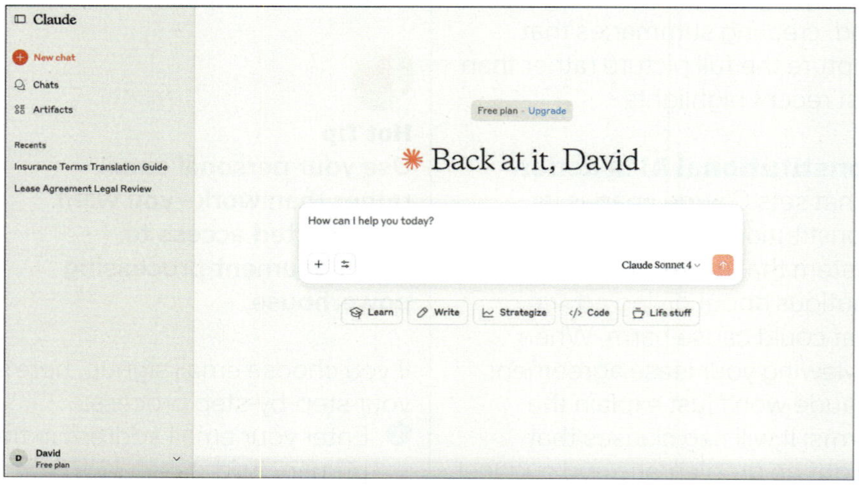

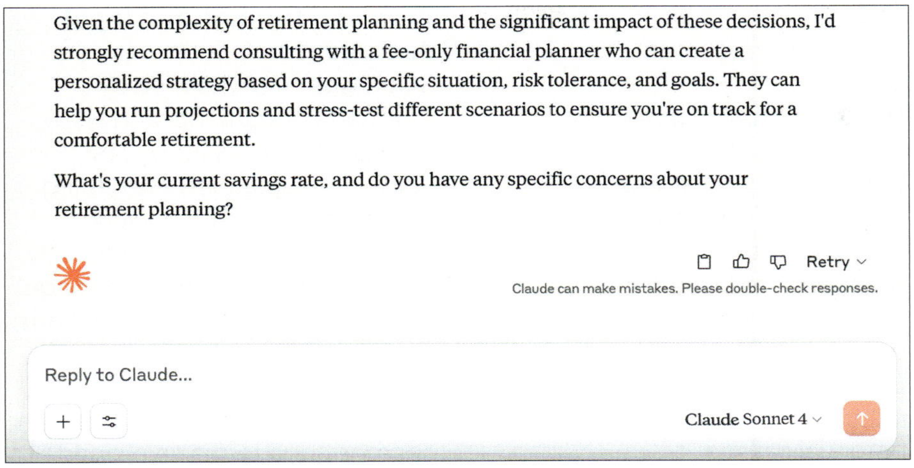

feedback during document processing:

- **Upload Progress** shows a clean progress bar while files process.
- **Processing Complete** displays a checkmark when Claude has fully analyzed your document.
- **File Type Recognition** shows icons indicating what type of document Claude detected.

Workflow organization that works

New Chat Strategy: Start fresh conversations for different document categories. Keep "Insurance Policies" separate from "Work Contracts", and separate from "Home Purchase Documents". Claude maintains better focus when conversations stay topically related.

File Management: Unlike other AI tools, Claude excels at handling multiple related documents in a single conversation. Upload your lease agreement, then add the HOA bylaws, then include the inspection report—Claude maintains context across all files.

Conversation Continuity: Claude remembers everything within a conversation, including previously uploaded documents. This means you can ask follow-up questions hours or even days later without re-uploading files or repeating context.

Next Level

Name your conversations immediately after uploading important documents—"2025 Home Insurance Review" beats "Chat with Claude" when you need to find it later.

Interface mastered. Now, you're ready to put Claude's document-processing capabilities to work on real challenges that have been sitting in your Downloads folder.

Your document-processing powerhouse

Claude transforms how you handle the paperwork that clutters modern life. Instead of struggling through dense legal language or corporate jargon, you can have an intelligent conversation about what these documents actually mean for you.

Contract and policy analysis

Upload your lease agreement, employment contract, or insurance policy, and Claude breaks down the dense legal language into plain English. It identifies key dates, obligations, and potential gotchas that could affect you later. More importantly, it explains the practical implications of each clause.

Ask specific questions like "What happens if I need to break this lease early?" or "Am I covered if my basement floods?". Claude will point you to the relevant sections and explain them in context. It can even flag unusual clauses that might warrant professional review.

Unlike generic document summarizers, Claude understands the relationships between different sections of your contract. It knows that the termination clause affects the security deposit terms, and that the maintenance responsibilities connect to the liability coverage.

Research and summarization

Academic papers, industry reports, and technical documentation become accessible when Claude processes them for you. It doesn't just create bullet-point summaries—it explains the research methodology, puts findings in context, and highlights practical applications you can actually use.

For professionals staying current in their fields, Claude transforms overwhelming reading lists into manageable insights. Feed it multiple research papers on a topic, and it will synthesize the findings, identify areas of agreement and disagreement, and suggest what the research means in practice.

Content transformation

Claude excels at converting formal documents into accessible formats. That 20-page compliance manual becomes a friendly FAQ. Dense technical specifications become clear user guides. Board meeting minutes transform into action-oriented summaries that people actually read.

This isn't just reformatting—Claude understands audience and purpose. Tell it you need content for new employees versus senior management, and the tone, detail level, and focus will shift accordingly.

Next Level

Try chain prompting—first ask for a summary, then ask "Now create a checklist of action items based on that summary".

Claude's unique features

What makes Claude particularly valuable isn't just what it can do, but how it approaches complex information challenges. These capabilities expand your options for tackling documents that other AI tools struggle with.

Advanced context understanding

Claude's 200,000-word context window means it can process entire books, complete policy manuals, or multiple related documents simultaneously. More importantly, it maintains understanding across all that content, making connections that shorter-context AI tools miss entirely.

This capability shines when working with complex legal documents that reference multiple sections, or when comparing different versions of the same policy. Claude tracks cross-references, identifies contradictions, and explains how changes in one section affect other parts of the document.

Multi-format processing

Upload CSV files, and Claude becomes your data interpreter. It can identify trends, explain unusual patterns, and translate numbers into insights. Ask "What's driving the increase in our customer service calls?" and Claude will analyze the data, identify patterns, and suggest potential causes.

Claude doesn't just crunch numbers—it puts them in context. It will notice that your highest sales months correlate with specific marketing campaigns, or that customer complaints spike after product updates. These connections help you move from data to decisions.

Visual document analysis

Upload photos of forms, receipts, handwritten notes, or diagrams, and Claude can extract and process the information. Snap a picture of a restaurant receipt for expense reporting, or photograph meeting notes from a whiteboard session.

This visual processing extends Claude's reach beyond digital documents. Insurance claims, medical forms, or handwritten contracts become as accessible as typed documents. Claude can even work with complex diagrams, flowcharts, and technical drawings.

Real-world usage stories

Real people across different life stages are using Claude's document skills to solve everyday problems. These stories show how document processing translates into practical benefits.

Personal finance and legal documents

Sarah was overwhelmed by mortgage documents and HOA bylaws when buying her first home. She uploaded everything to Claude and asked specific questions: "What are my monthly obligations beyond the mortgage payment?" and "What renovations require HOA approval?".

Claude identified hidden fees in her mortgage terms, explained HOA restrictions that would affect her planned garden renovation, and flagged a clause about special assessments that her realtor had missed. Armed with this understanding, Sarah negotiated better terms and avoided costly mistakes.

Did You Know?

Claude can remember context from earlier in your conversation, so you can build complex analysis step by step.

Robert, a recent retiree, needed to understand his retirement account statements, Medicare supplement options, and long-term care insurance policies. The financial industry's complex language was intimidating, but Claude made it manageable.

Claude explained how different withdrawal strategies would affect his tax burden, compared Medicare supplement plans based on his specific health needs, and identified the most cost-effective long-term care coverage for his situation.

Small business applications

Marcus runs a small consulting firm and was drowning in client contracts and vendor agreements.

Claude became his contract review assistant, identifying inconsistent payment terms, flagging unusual liability clauses, and creating standardized summaries for his files.

Now, Marcus uploads every contract to Claude first, asking "What's different about this agreement compared with my standard terms?". This process caught a client trying to extend payment terms from 30 to 90 days—a change that would have seriously affected cash flow.

Claude also helps Marcus create client-friendly summaries of complex project agreements, turning legal jargon into clear explanations of deliverables, timelines, and responsibilities that clients actually understand.

Academic and professional research

Elena, a graduate student in public policy, uses Claude to process academic papers and government reports. Instead of spending hours reading papers that might not be relevant, she uploads them to Claude for initial screening.

Claude identifies key findings, methodology concerns, and practical applications, helping Elena decide which papers deserve deeper study. For Elena's thesis research, Claude synthesized findings from dozens of studies, identifying patterns and gaps that shaped her research direction.

Dr. Martinez, a healthcare administrator, relies on Claude to process complex regulatory updates and policy changes. Claude translates dense government documents into actionable guidance for her staff, highlighting compliance requirements and implementation deadlines.

Project 1: policy to people-friendly

Ready to see Claude's document processing in action? These hands-on projects will let you put Claude through its paces.

Let's start by transforming a complex organizational policy into formats people will actually use—a staff-friendly FAQ and a concise poster for common areas.

Choosing your document

Start with a formal policy document between 1,500 and 3,000 words. Employee handbooks, remote work policies, benefits guides, or safety procedures work perfectly. The document should use formal, corporate language that real people find challenging to navigate.

If you don't have access to organizational policies, try user agreements from software you use, insurance policy documents, or HOA bylaws. The key is choosing something that affects you but feels impenetrable in its current form.

The upload process

Click the **Upload** button in Claude's interface and select your document. Claude accepts PDF, Word, and text files up to 25MB. While it processes, you'll see a progress indicator—large documents take 10-15 seconds to analyze.

1. Click upload area
2. Select your file
3. Wait for processing confirmation
4. Document appears in conversation

Crafting the perfect prompt

The magic happens in how you structure your request. Here's a proven template (RTF for Role, Task, Format) that gets excellent results every time:

Role: Perhaps a communications specialist would help us to understand company policies.

Task: We want the AI to make our remote work policy more accessible for all.

Format: We'll ask it for two usable outputs, a staff-friendly FAQ with 8 common questions, and a concise summary we might put on a poster.

Hot Tip
The RTF template works with any document—just adjust the Role and Format to match your specific needs and audience.

Multiple outputs from one request

What makes this approach powerful is getting multiple formats from a single conversation. Claude will read the entire policy once and create both outputs, ensuring consistency while optimizing each format for its intended purpose.

The FAQ addresses real questions with natural language answers. The poster format prioritizes the most important information in a visually scannable layout. Both serve different needs but draw from the same source material.

FAQ sample: *Q: Can I work from home whenever I want?*
A: You can work remotely up to 3 days per week, but you need to coordinate with your team and get approval for your regular schedule. Fridays require in-office presence for team meetings.

Poster sample: remote work quick reference
✓ Up to 3 days per week
✓ Team coordination required
✗ Manager approval needed
✗ Fridays must be in-office
✗ Client meeting days require office presence

Refinement techniques

Claude delivers excellent results that improve with specific refinement. Ask for targeted adjustments: "Make the FAQ more conversational" or "Add a section about equipment reimbursement to the poster".

You can also request different perspectives: "Now create a version of this FAQ that addresses manager concerns" or "Make a version of the poster that focuses on productivity expectations rather than logistics".

Project 2: contract comparison detective

Claude's ability to maintain context across long documents makes it perfect for side-by-side contract analysis. This project shows how to compare two similar agreements to spot the differences that matter.

Setting up your comparison

Find two related documents—different versions of the same contract, competing service agreements, or insurance policies from different companies. Property management agreements, cell phone contracts, or software licenses work perfectly for this exercise.

The key is choosing documents that serve similar purposes but come from different sources. You want to identify which terms favor you and which create potential problems.

The multi-document upload process

Upload both documents to Claude in the same conversation. Start with the first document, let Claude confirm it's processed, then upload the second. Claude will maintain context from both throughout your analysis.

Using SPARK for contract analysis

For more complex analysis, use the SPARK template—Scenario, Purpose, Actions, Results, Key Info:

Scenario: Maybe we have a rental property and want to choose a property management company.

Purpose: We have contracts from two companies and want to identify which one offers better terms, lower total costs, and more flexibility.

Actions: We'll ask for a side-by-side comparison...

Results: ...and a strong recommendation.

Key Info: We've got some specific areas we want to focus on.

Claude will read both documents completely, then create detailed comparisons that highlight differences in payment terms, cancellation policies, liability clauses, and other crucial elements. The SPARK framework ensures you get comprehensive analysis tailored to your specific decision-making needs.

Hot Tip
In this scenario, if you were unfamiliar with property management contracts you could first have a conversation with Claude to identify which areas are most critical to compare, and where there are common gotchas.

Deep-dive analysis questions

Once you have the basic comparison, ask targeted follow-up questions that leverage Claude's document comprehension:

"Which contract gives me more flexibility if my circumstances change?" Claude will reference specific clauses about modifications, transfers, and early termination across all your documents.

"Are there any hidden costs in either agreement that aren't immediately obvious?" Claude will identify fees buried in different sections and explain when they might apply.

"Which document has stronger consumer protections?" Claude will compare warranty terms, dispute resolution processes, and limitation of liability clauses.

Quick Start

Upload any two insurance quotes or service agreements and ask "Which one protects me better and costs less overall?".

Real-world application

Jennifer used this technique when choosing between two property management companies for her rental property. Claude compared their contracts and revealed that Company A's "lower" fee actually included expensive mandatory services that Company B offered as optional add-ons.

The analysis showed Company A would cost $3,600 more annually once all fees were calculated. Claude also identified that Company B's contract allowed Jennifer to terminate with 30 days' notice, while Company A required 90 days—a crucial difference she'd missed.

Advanced comparison techniques

For complex documents, try these sophisticated approaches:

Risk Assessment: "What are the biggest risks to me in each contract, and how likely are they to occur?"

Scenario Planning: "If I need to cancel early, move locations, or change my usage, how would each contract handle these situations?"

Hidden Dependencies: "Are there clauses in either contract that reference external policies or terms I should review?"

Claude's comprehensive understanding helps you move beyond surface-level comparisons to strategic decision-making. It connects related clauses, explains industry-standard practices, and flags unusual terms that deserve your attention.

This project demonstrates why Claude excels at document work—it's not just reading individual clauses, but understanding how different parts of complex agreements work together to create your overall obligations and protections.

Advanced techniques to achieve even more

Once you've mastered basic document processing, these advanced techniques separate power users from casual ones. They demonstrate Claude's sophisticated reasoning capabilities and help you build efficient document-processing systems.

Comparative analysis

Upload different versions of the same document and ask Claude to identify changes, assess improvements, or flag potential problems. This works excellently for contract revisions, policy updates, or comparing competing proposals.

Claude doesn't just list differences—it evaluates the implications of changes and helps you understand which modifications favor different parties or create new obligations.

Role-playing

Ask Claude to explain the same policy from different viewpoints: "How would a new employee interpret this policy versus how would a manager interpret it?" This technique reveals potential communication gaps and helps you anticipate any questions or concerns raised.

Next Level

Ask Claude to identify potential conflicts between different policies or sections within the same document.

Chain prompting

Build sophisticated analysis through sequential requests. Start with basic understanding, then layer on specific concerns: first ask for a summary, then ask about implementation challenges, then ask for a communication strategy.

Each response builds on previous analysis, creating deeper insights than you could get from a single request. This approach works particularly well for complex business documents where you need to understand multiple perspectives and implications.

These document-processing skills can also connect with your other digital tools and workflows. Export Claude's analysis to other apps, and use their inbuilt tools for further development of the content.

The key is thinking of Claude as part of a larger information processing system rather than a standalone tool.

Troubleshooting and pro tips

Even the most sophisticated AI encounters challenging documents. Understanding common issues and solutions helps you get consistent, high-quality results from Claude's document-processing capabilities.

When Claude gets confused

Complex documents with multiple sections, cross-references, or technical jargon can sometimes challenge even Claude's advanced processing. If you get a response that seems incomplete or off-target, try breaking your request into smaller pieces.

Instead of asking Claude to analyze an entire employee handbook, focus on specific sections: "Explain the vacation policy section" followed by "Now explain the remote work section". This approach helps Claude maintain focus and accuracy while building comprehensive understanding.

Warning

If Claude seems uncertain about important details, ask it to identify specific sections of the document that support its conclusions.

Prompt refinement

Specific language gets better results than general requests. Instead of "Summarize this document", try "Create a summary focusing on employee obligations and benefits, written for someone starting their first corporate job".

The simplicity of the RTF prompt template or the precision of the SPARK prompt template provide context about your situation. As you get familiar with this approach, you can explore alternative perspectives; for example, "I'm a department manager trying to explain this policy to my team" produces different results than "I'm an employee trying to understand my rights".

Working with sensitive information

Claude processes documents securely, but consider privacy implications when working with confidential information. For highly sensitive documents, you can paraphrase key sections rather than uploading complete files.

Claude can work with anonymized versions of documents where you replace specific names or amounts, or mark details with placeholders. This approach lets you get the analysis you need while protecting sensitive information.

Building document libraries

Claude remembers context within individual conversations, letting you build complex analysis step by step. Upload multiple related documents and have Claude compare them, identify contradictions, or synthesize information across sources.

This memory capability makes Claude particularly valuable for ongoing projects where you need to reference previous analysis or build understanding incrementally. Create comprehensive document analysis by layering insights from multiple sources in a single conversation.

Your document mastery journey starts now

You've just completed two real projects—more than most people do in their first month with Claude. That employee handbook? Start uploading it tonight. Those competing contracts? You're ready to spot the gotchas that could cost you thousands. The dense policy manual? Transform it into something people will actually want to read.

This is just your first taste. Claude can help you analyze medical bills, decode insurance policies, even turn complex research papers into actionable insights. The key? Start using it daily for document challenges—lease reviews, contract comparisons, policy explanations. Every interaction teaches you how to ask better questions and get deeper analysis.

Remember: Claude isn't about replacing your judgment—it's about making complex information accessible. You bring the context, priorities, and final decisions. Claude brings tireless attention to detail, and the ability to explain anything in plain English. Together? That's where document mastery happens.

Next Level

Keep a running conversation with Claude for ongoing document projects—it remembers everything and builds deeper understanding over time.

Tomorrow morning, grab that intimidating document you've been avoiding. Upload it to Claude with your coffee. Ask it to explain the three most important things you need to know. Start that conversation. Your patient, detail-obsessed reading companion is waiting to tackle whatever paperwork life throws at you. ■

Perplexity—your personal research assistant

Your doctor hands you a diagnosis you can't understand. Or maybe you're house hunting and need to research school districts, crime rates, and flood zones before making the biggest purchase of your life. The old approach meant opening 20 browser tabs, cross-referencing conflicting information, and wondering which sources you can trust.

Enter Perplexity AI—the research assistant that doesn't just give you answers, but shows you where those answers come from, and recommendations on top. Think of it as having a brilliant, energetic graduate student, able to read the entire internet in seconds, then present you with a perfectly organized report complete with citations.

Meet your research partner

Perplexity represents a fundamental shift in how we find information online. While Google serves up links for you to click through, and ChatGPT offers educated guesses based on past learning, Perplexity combines the best of both worlds. It searches the web in real time, reads multiple sources, and then delivers conversational answers with transparent citations.

Under the hood

Perplexity is an AI-powered search engine that functions more like a research assistant than a traditional search tool. Instead of showing you a list of websites to visit, it reads those websites for you, synthesizes the information, and presents you with a comprehensive answer in plain English.

Think of it as the evolution of search. Traditional search engines were designed for the early internet, when finding any relevant website was the challenge. Today, with billions of web pages available, the challenge isn't finding information—it's making sense of conflicting, outdated, or unreliable sources.

Perplexity solves this by acting as your intelligent filter. It evaluates sources for credibility, cross-references information across multiple sites, and presents you with synthesized answers that save hours of manual research.

How the research engine works

When you ask Perplexity a question, several sophisticated processes happen simultaneously. The AI first analyzes your question to understand what type of information you're seeking, then formulates multiple search queries to gather comprehensive data from across the web.

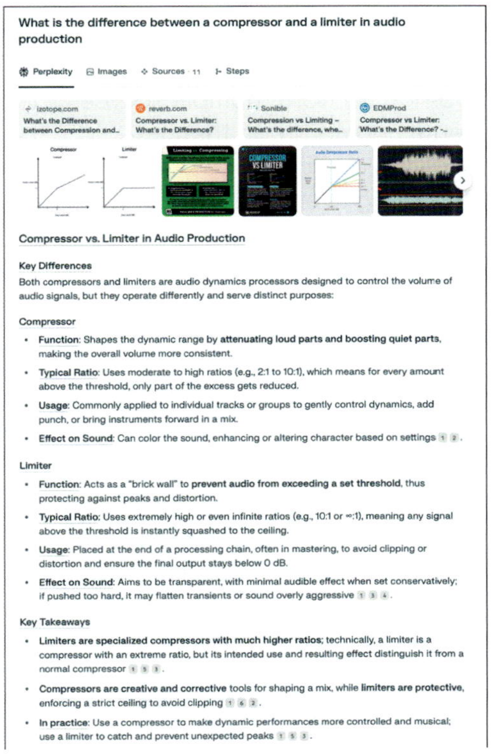

What is the difference between a compressor and a limiter in audio production

Perplexity | Images | Sources · 11 | Steps

izotope.com — What's the Difference between Compression and...
reverb.com — Compressor vs. Limiter: What's the Difference?
Sonible — Compression vs Limiting – What's the difference, whe...
EDMProd — Compressor vs Limiter: What's the Difference? -...

Compressor vs. Limiter in Audio Production

Key Differences

Both compressors and limiters are audio dynamics processors designed to control the volume of audio signals, but they operate differently and serve distinct purposes:

Compressor

- Function: Shapes the dynamic range by **attenuating loud parts and boosting quiet parts**, making the overall volume more consistent.
- Typical Ratio: Uses moderate to high ratios (e.g., 2:1 to 10:1), which means for every amount above the threshold, only part of the excess gets reduced.
- Usage: Commonly applied to individual tracks or groups to gently control dynamics, add punch, or bring instruments forward in a mix.
- Effect on Sound: Can color the sound, enhancing or altering character based on settings 1 2.

Limiter

- Function: Acts as a "brick wall" to **prevent audio from exceeding a set threshold**, thus protecting against peaks and distortion.
- Typical Ratio: Uses extremely high or even infinite ratios (e.g., 10:1 or ∞:1), meaning any signal above the threshold is instantly squashed to the ceiling.
- Usage: Placed at the end of a processing chain, often in mastering, to avoid clipping or distortion and ensure the final output stays below 0 dB.
- Effect on Sound: Aims to be transparent, with minimal audible effect when set conservatively; if pushed too hard, it may flatten transients or sound overly aggressive 1 3 4.

Key Takeaways

- **Limiters are specialized compressors with much higher ratios**; technically, a limiter is a compressor with an extreme ratio, but its intended use and resulting effect distinguish it from a normal compressor 1 5 3.
- **Compressors are creative and corrective** tools for shaping a mix, while **limiters are protective**, enforcing a strict ceiling to avoid clipping 1 6 2.
- In practice: Use a compressor to make dynamic performances more controlled and musical; use a limiter to catch and prevent unexpected peaks 1 5 3.

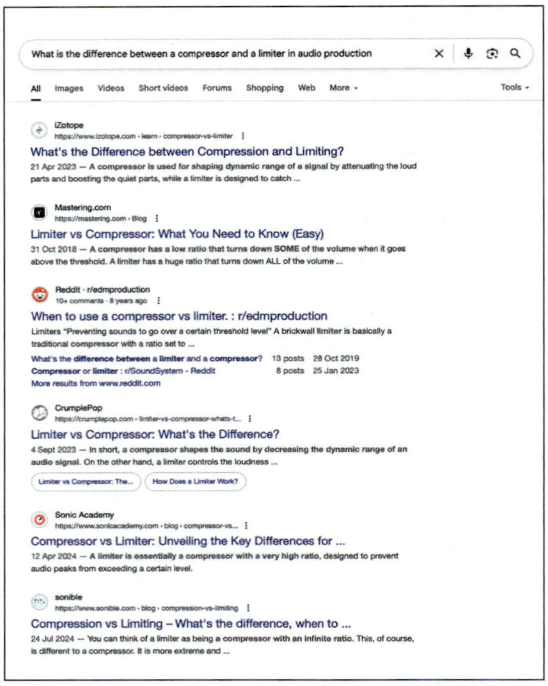
What is the difference between a compressor and a limiter in audio production

All Images Videos Short videos Forums Shopping Web More Tools

iZotope
https://www.izotope.com › learn › compressor-vs-limiter
What's the Difference between Compression and Limiting?
21 Apr 2023 — A compressor is used for shaping dynamic range of a signal by attenuating the loud parts and boosting the quiet parts, while a limiter is designed to catch ...

Mastering.com
https://mastering.com › Blog
Limiter vs Compressor: What You Need to Know (Easy)
31 Oct 2018 — A compressor has a low ratio that turns down SOME of the volume when it goes above the threshold. A limiter has a huge ratio that turns down ALL of the volume ...

Reddit · r/edmproduction
10+ comments · 8 years ago
When to use a compressor vs limiter. : r/edmproduction
Limiters "Preventing sounds to go over a certain threshold level" A brickwall limiter is basically a traditional compressor with a ratio set to ...
What's the difference between a limiter and a compressor? 13 posts 28 Oct 2019
Compressor or limiter : r/SoundSystem - Reddit 8 posts 25 Jan 2023
More results from www.reddit.com

CrumplePop
https://crumplepop.com › limiter-vs-compressor-whats-t...
Limiter vs Compressor: What's the Difference?
4 Sept 2023 — In short, a compressor shapes the sound by decreasing the dynamic range of an audio signal. On the other hand, a limiter controls the loudness ...
Limiter vs Compressor: The... How Does a Limiter Work?

Sonic Academy
https://www.sonicacademy.com › blog › compressor-vs...
Compressor vs Limiter: Unveiling the Key Differences for ...
12 Apr 2024 — A limiter is essentially a compressor with a very high ratio, designed to prevent audio peaks from exceeding a certain level.

sonible
https://www.sonible.com › blog › compression-vs-limiting
Compression vs Limiting – What's the difference, when to ...
24 Jul 2024 — You can think of a limiter as being a compressor with an infinite ratio. This, of course, is different to a compressor. It is more extreme and ...

As it searches, Perplexity evaluates source quality, checking for factors like publication date and author credibility, and cross-references with other reliable sources. This isn't just keyword matching—it's intelligent content analysis that understands context and relevance.

The AI then synthesizes information from multiple sources, identifying common themes, resolving contradictions, and organizing everything into a coherent response. Every claim in that response links back to its original source, creating a transparent trail you can verify.

Did You Know?
Perplexity often finds sources that don't appear on Google's first page, including academic papers, local news sites, and specialized databases.

Why Perplexity stands out

The research landscape is crowded with tools promising to revolutionize how we find information. Perplexity stands apart through three key innovations that address the core frustrations of modern research.

Real-time web access changes everything

Unlike AI models trained on older data, Perplexity searches the web as you ask. This means you get current restaurant reviews, today's flight prices, and this week's political developments. For any research that affects real decisions—from vacation planning to investment choices—this timeliness proves invaluable.

Consider researching "best restaurants in Chicago". ChatGPT might recommend places that closed during the pandemic, while Perplexity will find restaurants that opened last month, complete with recent reviews and current menu prices.

This real-time capability extends beyond simple facts to complex analysis. Ask about "current mortgage rates and market predictions", and you'll receive information based on this week's financial reports, not last year's training data.

Did You Know?
Perplexity indexes over 10 billion web pages and updates its search results every few minutes, compared with traditional search engines that may take days or weeks to index new content.

Citation transparency builds trust

The citation system builds trust in a way other AI tools can't match. Every claim in Perplexity's answer links directly to its source, letting you verify important information and dive deeper when needed. This transparency transforms AI from a "black box" into a research tool you can actually rely on.

When Perplexity tells you that "property values in Austin increased 12% this year", you can click directly to the real estate report that contains this data. This isn't just convenient—it's essential for any decision involving significant money, health, or life changes.

The Sources panel also reveals the quality of information behind each answer. You'll quickly learn to trust responses backed by multiple reputable sources while remaining skeptical of claims supported only by single blog posts or forums.

Tool	Citations	Conversation threading	Answer quality	Best for...
Perplexity	Yes (inline)	Yes	Excellent summaries	Deep "source explorer" sidebar
Bing Chat	Yes (clear links)	Yes	Good quality	Built straight into Edge browser
You.com	Yes (mixed)	Yes	Good, but variable	Privacy-first, ad-free experience
Google Search	No	No	High	Ubiquitous index of the entire web
Neeva AI	Yes (clean UI)	No	Very focused answers	Ad-free subscription model

Comparison advantage over competitors

Traditional search engines excel at finding specific websites but struggle with synthesis. AI chatbots provide confident answers but often can't verify their claims. Search engines with AI integration, like Bing Chat, offer some citation features but lack Perplexity's focus and refinement. Perplexity's conversation threading also surpasses competitors. Follow-up questions maintain full context, allowing you to build complex research projects. This turns research from a series of isolated searches into a coherent precise investigation.

Hot Tip

Bookmark conversations about ongoing research projects. Perplexity maintains the full context, making it easy to continue where you left off.

Perplexity vs. traditional research methods

Understanding how Perplexity transforms the research process reveals why millions have adopted this tool for everything from homework to major life decisions.

The old way: tab overload and information chaos

Traditional web research follows a predictable, frustrating pattern. You start with a Google search, open several promising links in new tabs, read through each website looking for relevant information, then attempt to piece together a coherent understanding from many different sources.

This approach creates several problems. First, you waste enormous amounts of time clicking through websites that don't actually contain the information you need. Second, you struggle to evaluate source credibility without extensive background knowledge. Third, you often miss crucial information because you can't read every relevant source on the web.

Time savings that actually matter

Perplexity eliminates the tab explosion by reading multiple sources for you. What used to take 45 minutes of clicking and reading now takes 5 minutes of focused questioning. This isn't just about speed—it's about thoroughness.

When researching "sustainable investing options", traditional search might lead you to read three or four articles from financial websites. Perplexity reads dozens of sources—recent academic papers, current market reports, regulatory updates, and expert analyses—then synthesizes this information into a comprehensive overview.

The time savings compound when you need to research multiple related topics. Traditional research requires starting over with each new question. Perplexity's conversation threading lets you build on previous answers, creating a research session that grows more sophisticated with each exchange.

Quality control: when sources actually matter

Traditional research puts the burden of source evaluation entirely on you. Unless you're already an expert in the field, distinguishing between credible and questionable sources becomes guesswork. Perplexity's AI evaluation helps by prioritizing recent, authoritative sources and cross-referencing claims across multiple publications.

This quality control proves especially valuable for complex topics where misinformation spreads easily. Health information, financial advice, and technical recommendations all benefit from Perplexity's ability to identify and weight credible sources appropriately.

Getting your research lab set up

Creating your Perplexity account takes less time than making coffee, but the impact on your research capabilities will last much longer.

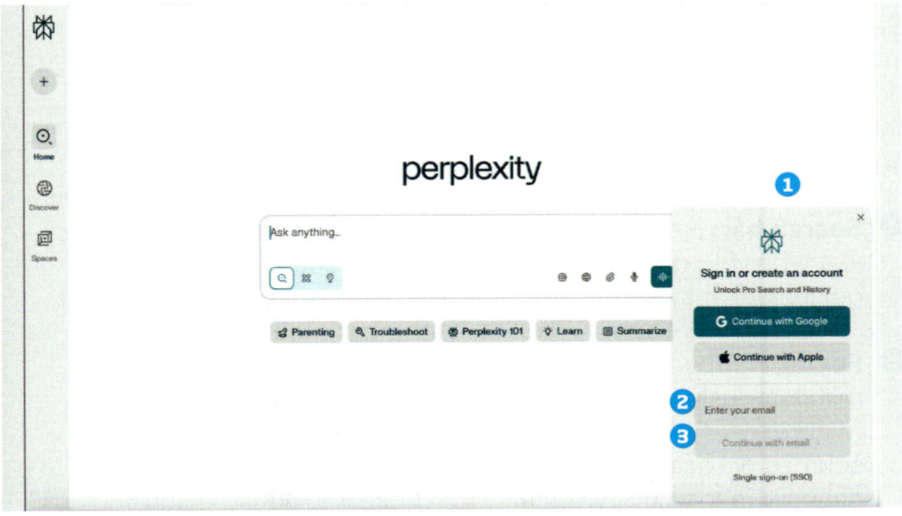

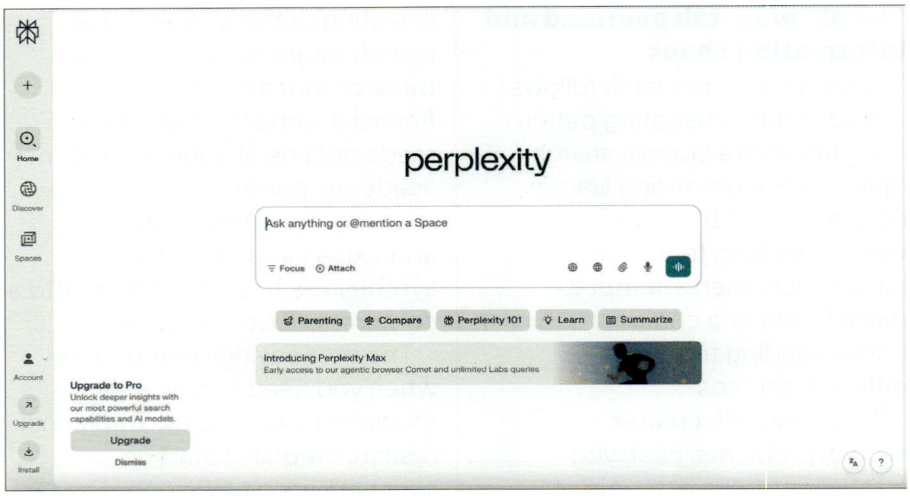

Creating your account

Visit **perplexity.ai**.

1. Choose between using your *Google* or *Apple* account, or signing up with an email address

If using email:

2. Enter your email address in the **Email** field and click **Continue with email**
3. Check your email for a one-time code or temporary sign-in link

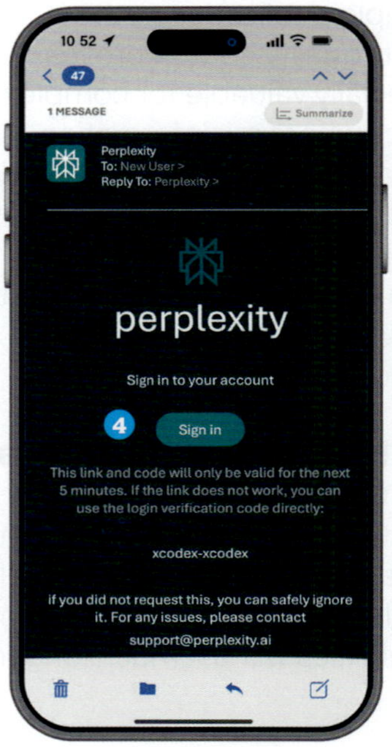

4. Click **Sign in** or copy the code and paste it into the **Enter code** field on the **Check your email** page
5. On the **Select your plan** page, click on **Continue with free**
6. On the **Use Perplexity anywhere you ask questions** page, click on **Continue**

The free tier gives you substantial research power with unlimited basic searches. This provides more than enough capability for most research needs, from travel planning to academic projects.

First steps in your dashboard

Once you're in, you'll notice Perplexity's deliberately clean interface. The prominent Search bar dominates the screen, reinforcing that this tool prioritizes getting you answers over flashy features.

1. **Search bar:** Front and center—just type your questions and get instant answers
2. **Focus:** Narrow down your results by using the Focus feature to target specific sources like academic journals or social media
3. **File upload:** Drag and drop a document into the Search bar and ask Perplexity for quick insights
4. **Pro Search:** For a deeper dive, Pro Search pulls from a broader range of sources to give you more in-depth information. Free users can use Pro Search five times every four hours, while Pro subscribers get nearly unlimited access
5. **Sidebar:** You can easily access your search history, save important queries in Collections, browse trending topics in Discover, and adjust your settings

The sidebar shows your recent conversations, making it easy to return to previous research sessions. Each conversation maintains context, so you can ask follow-up questions without repeating background information.

Quick Start

Bookmark Perplexity.ai and consider adding it to your browser's search engines for quick access.

Your research mission control

Perplexity's interface reveals its power gradually. What looks simple on the surface contains sophisticated features that transform how you gather and analyze information.

The power features

The search experience begins when you type your question. Unlike traditional search engines

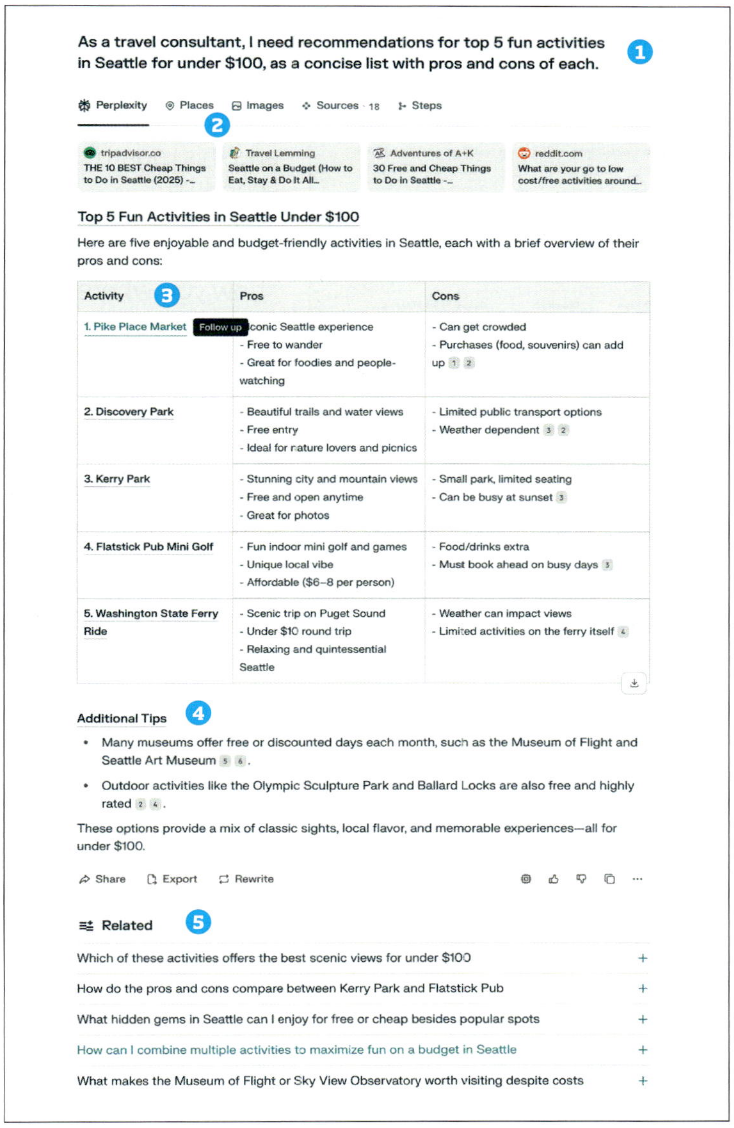

that expect keywords, Perplexity thrives on complete, detailed questions. The more context you provide, the better your results.

As Perplexity researches your question, you'll see sources appear in real time on the right-hand side of your screen. This transparency lets you watch the AI build its answer, showing which websites, articles, and databases it's consulting.

1. Search input
2. AI response being generated
3. Source citations appearing
4. Follow-up questions
5. Related topics suggested

Hidden gems you'll love

After delivering your answer, Perplexity suggests related questions you might want to explore. These suggestions often reveal angles you hadn't considered, making your research more thorough.

The Sources panel ranks results by relevance and recency, with newer information typically appearing first. You can click any source to read the full article, then return to continue your research conversation.

The conversation history feature transforms scattered research

into organized projects. Name your conversations clearly—"Denver Housing Research" or "Mediterranean Diet Studies"—and you can return to continue your investigation weeks later.

Hot Tip

Save important conversations by clicking the Bookmark icon. This creates a searchable archive of your research projects.

Two smart ways to ask better questions

The difference between mediocre and exceptional research often comes down to how you frame your questions. Two proven methods will transform your Perplexity results.

The RTF method: Research, Target, Focus

For everyday questions, use the RTF framework: Research + Target + Focus. This structure gives Perplexity clear boundaries while keeping your query concise.

Research: The topic you're wanting to explore.

Target: Your specific criteria or constraints.

Focus: The most important factors for your decision.

This approach works because it prevents Perplexity from delivering generic information. Instead of getting a broad overview of electric vehicles, you receive targeted recommendations that match your exact situation.

Warning

Avoid vague questions like "What's the best car?". Instead, specify your needs, budget, and priorities.

The SPARK method: for serious research

When facing complex decisions—buying a home, choosing medical treatments, or making career changes—use the SPARK method:

Situation: Your current circumstances.

Purpose: What you're trying to accomplish.

Audience: Who's affected by this decision.

Requirements: Must-have criteria.

Key Questions: Specific concerns you need addressed.

This comprehensive approach ensures Perplexity understands the full context of your research wants and needs.

As a travel consultant, I want a suggested itinerary for a weekend trip to Austin...

Perplexity · Images · Sources · 10

Here is a suggested **weekend itinerary for a couple's trip to Austin, Texas in November**, focusing on walkable neighborhoods, food, and live music. The plan prioritizes the vibrant areas of Downtown, South Congress, and East Austin, where you'll find a blend of culinary hotspots and iconic music venues. November weather is typically mild, making Austin's walkable neighborhoods especially enjoyable [2] [6].

Time	Activity & Venue	Neighborhood	Notes
Friday			
Afternoon	Check in at a boutique hotel (e.g., Heywood Hotel or downtown option)	East Austin/Downtown	Central location for walking to food and music spots [2].
Evening	Dinner at Lambert's (upscale BBQ + live music upstairs)	Downtown	Classic Texas BBQ in a stylish setting [4].
Night	Live music bar hop on Sixth Street (Antone's, Townsend, etc.)	Downtown	Legendary venues with nightly live music [2].
Saturday			
Morning	Breakfast tacos at Veracruz All Natural or Jo's Coffee	South Congress/East	Iconic Austin breakfast experience [2].
Late Morning	Stroll South Congress Avenue (SoCo): boutiques, murals, and coffee shops	South Congress	Walkable, lively, and full of Austin character [2].
Lunch	Food truck park or Banger's Beer Garden (sausages, craft beer, live music)	Rainey Street	Rainey is known for food trucks and quirky bars [6].
Afternoon	Art at Blanton Museum of Art	UT/Downtown	Inspiring collection, easy walk from downtown [1].
Sunset	Rooftop cocktails at P6 (The Line Hotel)	Downtown/Lady Bird	Stunning city and lake views [1].
Evening	Dinner at Comedor (modern Mexican, innovative menu)	Downtown	Stylish, contemporary dining [1].
Night	Live music & dancing at The Continental Club	South Congress	Iconic, intimate venue for local music and dancing [1].
Sunday			
Morning	Brunch at 1886 Café & Bakery or Justine's (French bistro, romantic)	Downtown/East Austin	Both offer great food and ambiance [2] [3].
Late Morning	Walk Lady Bird Lake Trail or kayak on the lake	Downtown	Scenic, relaxing outdoor activity [1] [10].
Lunch	Picnic at Mount Bonnell (city views, stargazing if time allows)	Northwest	Romantic and peaceful end to the trip [1].

Additional Tips:

- For live music, check the current schedules at Antone's, The Continental Club, and Rainey Street bars as lineups change weekly [2] [6].
- Most venues and neighborhoods listed are highly walkable, especially Downtown, South Congress, and Rainey Street [2] [6].
- For wine lovers, Wanderlust Wine Co. offers self-serve wine flights and cheese boards, ideal for a relaxed afternoon or pre-dinner stop [1].

This itinerary blends Austin's renowned food scene and live music culture with the city's most walkable and atmospheric neighborhoods, ensuring a memorable weekend for couples [1] [2] [6].

Project 1: weekend trip research

Let's put the RTF method into action with a practical example that demonstrates Perplexity's real-time capabilities.

Your mission

Research a weekend trip to Austin, Texas, in November, focusing on current recommendations rather than outdated travel guides.

What you'll get

Perplexity will search current restaurant reviews, November event calendars, and recent visitor experiences. Unlike static travel websites, you'll receive information about which venues are actually open, current menu highlights, and this month's live music schedule.

The Sources panel will show you where each recommendation comes from—recent TripAdvisor reviews, local event websites, and Austin food blogs. This transparency lets you evaluate the credibility of each suggestion.

Following up like a pro

After receiving your initial answer, ask targeted follow-up questions:

- "What are the walking distances between these recommended restaurants?"
- "Which live music venues have shows on Saturday nights in November?"
- "What's the current average cost for dinner at these recommended places?"

Next Level

Screenshot or copy key findings into a note-taking app with the source links for easy reference during your trip.

Project 2: the big decision research

Now, let's tackle something more complex using the SPARK method—researching solar panel installation for your home.

Building your SPARK prompt

Situation: Homeowner in Phoenix, Arizona, considering solar panels

for energy independence and cost savings.

Purpose: Understand current costs, financing options, and installation process to make an informed long-term investment.

Audience: Making this decision affects your family's budget and home value.

Requirements: Current pricing, reputable local installers, financing options, maintenance needs.

Key Questions: What's the typical ROI timeline? How does this affect property values? What maintenance is required?

Working with the results

Perplexity will provide current pricing from multiple sources, local installer recommendations with recent customer reviews, and up-to-date information about federal and Arizona state incentives.

Pay attention to the source diversity—credible responses should include recent news articles about pricing trends, local installer websites, government energy websites, and consumer review platforms.

Follow up with specific questions about the installers Perplexity recommends:

- "What do recent customers say about [installer name] in Phoenix?"
- "What warranties do these companies typically offer?"
- "How do current Arizona solar incentives compare to federal programs?"

When things go wrong (and how to fix them)

Even the best research tool occasionally delivers subpar results. Here's how to troubleshoot common issues and get better answers:

Sources seem outdated

If Perplexity pulls information from older articles, refine your search with time-based keywords. Add "current", "2025", or "recent developments" to your query. For rapidly changing topics, specify "latest news" or "this month".

The phrase "based on recent reports" signals to Perplexity that you want the newest available information. For evolving situations like market conditions or health guidelines, this specificity makes a significant difference.

Hot Tip

If you get irrelevant results, try starting your question with "According to recent sources" or "Based on current information" to signal that recency matters.

Answers too general?

Vague results usually stem from vague questions. Return to the RTF or SPARK structure and add specific details about location, timeframe, budget, or personal requirements.

Instead of "What's the best smartphone?" ask "Research smartphones under $800 for photography enthusiasts who travel frequently. Target models with excellent low-light cameras and long battery life. Focus on current 2025 models with positive user reviews.".

Can't find what you need?

Sometimes the problem isn't Perplexity—it's your question format. Try rephrasing statements as questions, or break complex topics into smaller, more focused queries.

If you're researching "sustainable investing strategies", start with "What are the main types of sustainable investing?", then follow up with "How do ESG funds typically perform compared to traditional funds?".

Research ethics matter too. When Perplexity provides information for important decisions, verify key facts by clicking through to original sources. AI synthesis is powerful, but your critical thinking remains essential.

Hot Tip

If Perplexity can't find current information, your topic might be too new, too niche, or too localized for web sources.

Warning

Always verify medical, financial, or legal information with qualified professionals. Perplexity provides research starting points and not professional advice.

Level up your research game

Once you're comfortable with basic Perplexity searches, these advanced techniques will make your research more efficient and comprehensive.

Master the follow-up

Perplexity's conversation threading lets you build complex research projects over multiple queries. Each follow-up question maintains context from previous exchanges, allowing you to dive deeper without repeating background information.

After researching "best meditation apps for beginners", follow up with "Which of these apps work offline?" or "What do users say about the price of the subscription costs?".

Use the power phrase "What else should I consider?" to uncover blind spots in your research. This often reveals important factors you hadn't thought to investigate.

The conversation history becomes your research journal. For significant decisions, you can trace your entire investigation process, see how your understanding evolved, and find out which sources influenced your thinking.

Compare like a pro

For any decision involving multiple options, use Perplexity's comparison capabilities. Frame requests as "Compare X vs Y for [specific use case]" to get structured analysis.

"Compare Notion vs. Obsidian for academic researchers who work with large amounts of text and need robust linking features."

Request pros and cons lists with sources: "What are the advantages and disadvantages of living in Portland vs. Seattle for remote workers, based on recent resident experiences?".

Perplexity excels at synthesizing comparison data from multiple sources, giving you balanced perspectives that would take hours to compile manually.

Advanced search operators and filters

While Perplexity doesn't use traditional search operators like Google, you can guide its research with strategic phrasing. Use "according to academic sources" for scholarly information, "based on user reviews" for consumer perspectives, or "from government reports" for official data.

Time-based qualifiers work particularly well: "in the last six months", "recent studies show", or "current industry reports" help Perplexity prioritize newer information. For local research, specify geographic boundaries: "in the San Francisco Bay area" or "for US residents" ensures relevant results every time.

Stay organized

Use Perplexity's conversation history strategically. Name your research sessions clearly—"Solar Panel Research March 2025" or "Austin Trip Planning"—so that you can find them later.

For important research projects, take screenshots of key findings and copy crucial information with source links into your preferred note-taking app.

Your first research win

The best way to appreciate Perplexity's capabilities is to tackle a real research project this week. Start with something you're genuinely curious about—a vacation destination, a purchase you're considering, or a skill you want to learn.

Next Level

Create a research template in your note-taking app with sections for Perplexity findings, source links, follow-up questions, and final decisions.

Choose your practice project

Select a research topic that genuinely matters to your current life. This might be comparing health insurance plans, researching a potential career change, or planning a significant purchase. The investment in learning Perplexity pays off when you apply it to real decisions.

Begin with the RTF method for straightforward questions. As you grow comfortable with the tool, graduate to SPARK when facing bigger decisions. The goal is building confidence with the interface and working on question-framing techniques.

Apply what you've learned

Start your research session with a clear, specific question using either an RTF or a SPARK structure. Pay attention to the sources Perplexity cites—this teaches you to recognize quality information sources in your field of interest.

Use follow-up questions to dig deeper into aspects that matter most to your decision. Remember that effective research is an iterative process. Your first question should lead to better follow-up questions, and Perplexity's conversation threading makes this natural exploration possible. ■

Paid vs. free—is the upgrade worth it?

You've been using ChatGPT for three weeks, and it just cut you off mid-conversation with that familiar "you've reached your limit" message. Your project deadline is tomorrow. Sound familiar?

This exact scenario plays out thousands of times daily as millions wrestle with whether AI subscriptions justify the cost when free versions exist. The answer isn't the same for everyone, but it's easier to figure out than you think.

What you actually get for your money

The marketing promises sound impressive, but what do paid AI subscriptions actually deliver beyond the free versions? The differences fall into two categories that matter most to real users.

Speed and availability when it counts

Free users get bumped to the back of the line during peak hours—exactly when you need AI most. Paid subscribers skip the queue entirely. ChatGPT Plus users get priority access even when servers are slammed. Claude Pro eliminates the daily message limits that stop conversations mid-stream. Perplexity Pro processes searches faster and handles more complex research requests without any delays.

Quick Start

Test the free version during your busiest work day—if you hit limits, you need the upgrade.

The real kicker? Free users often can't access AI when everyone else is trying to use it—weekday mornings, Sunday evenings, and deadline crunch times. Paid subscribers get consistent access regardless of traffic.

Advanced features that change the game

Premium subscriptions unlock capabilities that transform how you work with AI. Claude Pro handles documents up to 200 pages and remembers context across much longer conversations. ChatGPT Plus gives you access to GPT-4, and the ability to browse the web in real time and create custom GPTs tailored to your specific needs. Perplexity Pro searches academic databases and provides more detailed citations for research projects.

File uploads become game-changers for students and professionals. Upload a PDF, spreadsheet, or image and get instant analysis—something free versions either can't do or are severely limited in doing.

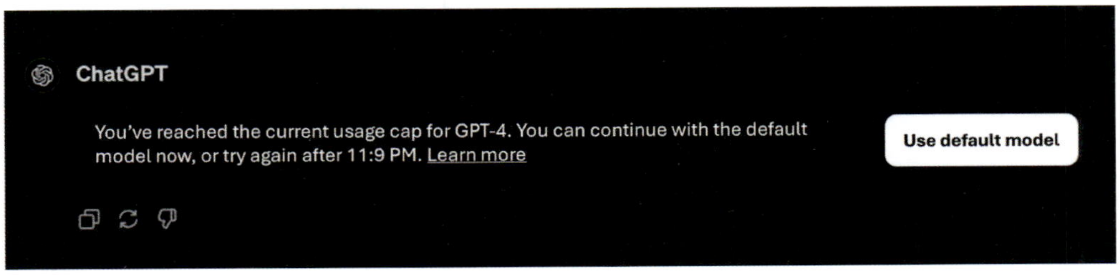

Feature	ChatGPT Free	ChatGPT Plus (*and above*)	Claude Free	Claude Pro (*and above*)	Perplexity Free	Perplexity Pro (*and above*)
Models (*at time of writing*)	GPT-4o & GPT-3.5	GPT-4	Claude Instant (v1.0)	Claude 2.1	Basic model	GPT-4-based engine
Context Window (*how much memory for a single chat*)	4 K tokens	32 K tokens	9 K tokens	75 K tokens	2 K tokens	8 K tokens
Costs	**Free**	**From $20 / month + higher tiers**	**Free**	**From $20 / month + higher tiers**	**Free**	**From $20 / month + higher tiers**
Usage Restrictions (*messages*)	GPT-4o limit / 5 hrs, GPT-3.5 unlimited	GPT-4o 80 msgs/3 hrs, GPT-4 40 msgs/3 hrs	40 msgs per day	45 msgs per 5 hours	5 msgs per day	300 msgs per day, Enterprise unlimited
Speed / Priority	Standard (*slower during peak*)	Priority access	Standard (*slower during peak*)	Faster throughput	Standard (*slower during peak*)	Priority routing
Customization	In-chat prompts only	Persistent prompts, Custom GPTs	No memory / persona settings	Memory & custom tweaks	None	Save & reuse prompts
History (*access past chats*)	30 days stored	90 days stored	Session only (*clears on reload*)	Saved & searchable threads	Last 10 chats	Unlimited saved transcripts
Plugins & API Access	✗	✓ Official plugins available ✗ (*API Dev Plan*)	✗	✗ (*Anthropic API*)	✗	✓ 50 K tokens per month
Privacy & Data Retention	May train on chats	Opt-out available	May learn from chats	"No-training" assurance	Queries logged	Ad-free; deletion on request
Support & SLA	Community forums	Email support	Community support	Priority email support	Email ticketing	Faster SLA response

The break-even point: when upgrades pay for themselves

Most AI subscriptions cost $15-$25 monthly. That's $0.50-$0.83 per day—less than your morning coffee. The math becomes straightforward when you calculate the time savings.

Time-is-money calculations

If you save two hours monthly using AI tools, most subscriptions pay for themselves. Here's the breakdown: AI helps you draft emails faster, research topics without endless scrolling, and brainstorm solutions when you're stuck. A student spending three hours researching for papers could cut that to one hour with unlimited AI access.

Hot Tip

Track your usage for one week—if you hit free limits more than twice, upgrade.

Small business owners see even clearer returns. A marketing consultant using AI to draft social media content, email campaigns, and blog outlines can bill clients for the time saved. The subscription pays for itself with the first saved hour.

Professional vs. personal use cases

Professional use demands reliability that free versions can't guarantee. Missing deadlines because AI hit daily limits costs more than any subscription.

Sales managers preparing client proposals can't risk losing momentum when researching competitor pricing at 2 PM on Tuesday.

Freelance writers meeting publication deadlines need guaranteed access when editors request last-minute revisions.

Graduate students analyzing literature for their thesis can't afford to lose access halfway through comparing research sources.

Social media managers posting daily content across multiple platforms hit free limits by noon during busy campaign weeks.

Personal users have different thresholds. Free versions will handle typical casual conversations and simple questions perfectly well.

Families planning summer vacations can research destinations and compare hotels over several weekends without hitting any limits.

Home cooks experimenting with new cuisines ask occasional questions about ingredient substitutions and cooking techniques.

Parents organizing family schedules create activity lists and chore charts during quiet evenings to maintain structure and reduce stress.

The line between personal and professional AI use isn't always clear-cut. What starts as a hobby or personal interest can quickly evolve into something that demands professional-level reliability. When your personal project starts generating income, affecting your reputation, or supporting your career goals, those "just for fun" AI conversations all of a sudden become mission-critical.

Side-hustle entrepreneurs building Etsy shops need reliable access when customer inquiries pile up during holiday seasons.

Aspiring writers exploring creative fiction brainstorm character ideas and plot developments sporadically.

Weekend photographers building Instagram followings hit limits when engaging with followers and planning content shoots.

Your personal upgrade decision tree

The upgrade decision comes down to matching your tool usage to your actual needs. Most people fall clearly into one of two camps once they honestly assess their patterns.

Stick with free if...

Casual exploration suits you perfectly. You ask AI occasional questions, experiment with creative writing prompts, or research topics sporadically. Free versions excel at answering straightforward questions, helping with basic brainstorming, and handling simple tasks.

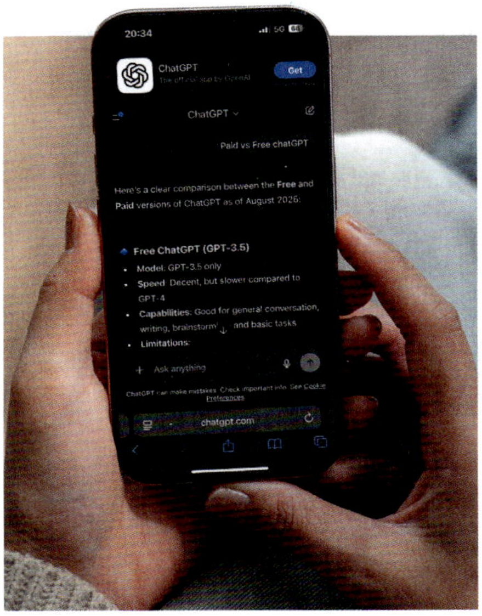

Budget constraints make subscriptions impractical, but you still want AI benefits. Free ChatGPT, Claude, and Perplexity provide substantial value without cost. You'll hit limits occasionally, but patience and timing can work around most restrictions.

Did You Know?

Most free AI users never hit daily limits because their usage is naturally sporadic.

Upgrading makes sense when...

Professional work depends on consistent AI access. Journalists researching stories, consultants creating presentations, and marketers developing campaigns can't afford interruptions. The reliability alone justifies the cost.

Student projects require deep research and long-form writing support. Analyzing literature, comparing research sources, and editing drafts all benefit from extended AI conversations that free versions cut short.

Creative pursuits become more ambitious with unlimited access. Writing novels, developing business ideas, or creating content for social media all flourish with unrestricted AI collaboration.

> **"Track your usage for seven days–if you hit limits twice, the upgrade pays for itself."**

Warning

Don't upgrade just because everyone else is—assess your actual usage patterns first.

Your next step: the seven-day test

Try this simple approach: use AI tools normally for one week while tracking every interaction. Note when you hit limits, feel frustrated by speed, or wish you could upload files. If limitations interrupt your workflow more than twice, upgrade makes financial sense.

The beauty of this decision? There's no wrong choice. Free AI tools provide incredible value for casual users, while paid subscriptions unlock professional-grade capabilities for power users. Match the tool to your needs, not the marketing hype, and you'll make the choice that actually works for your life. ■

Next Level

Start with one paid subscription to test the difference, then expand to others if the benefits prove worthwhile.

A roundup of other generative AI apps

You've mastered ChatGPT for brainstorming, Claude for document analysis, and Perplexity for research. But what happens when you need to turn your vacation photos into a professional slideshow, or create a podcast intro that doesn't sound like it was recorded in your bathroom?

The truth is, while the "Big Three" excel at conversation and text, specialized AI tools often outperform these generalists for specific creative and professional tasks. Think of it like choosing between a Swiss Army knife and a surgeon's scalpel—both have their place, but when precision matters, you want the right tool for the job.

The visual creators

The visual AI revolution has exploded beyond simple photo filters. Today's image generation tools create everything from marketing graphics to artistic masterpieces that rival human designers.

Text-to-image generators

Midjourney leads the pack for artistic image creation. Its *Discord*-based interface feels quirky at first, but the results speak for themselves. Type "/imagine a cozy coffee shop in watercolor style" and watch as it produces four stunning variations. The tool excels at understanding artistic styles and creating images with genuine aesthetic appeal.

DALL-E from OpenAI takes a more straightforward approach. Its web interface feels familiar, and it handles photorealistic images particularly well. Ask for "a golden retriever wearing sunglasses at a beach resort" and you'll get exactly that—no artistic interpretation required.

Stable Diffusion offers the open-source alternative. While it requires more technical know-how, it runs locally on your computer and gives you complete control over the process. Creative professionals love it for the customization possibilities.

Warning

Open-source AI tools like *Stable Diffusion* require technical setup and powerful computer hardware—check system requirements before downloading.

Photo editing gets smarter

Photoshop's AI features have transformed photo editing from hours-long projects into minutes-long tasks. The new Generative Fill tool lets you select any area and describe what you want to see there. Remove unwanted tourists from vacation photos or add a sunset to a gray sky—it's like having a professional retoucher on call.

Canva Magic Studio brings AI superpowers to everyday users. The Magic Eraser removes backgrounds instantly, while Magic Write generates social media captions that match your brand voice. Small business owners particularly love how it creates professional-looking marketing materials without design experience.

Lensa focuses specifically on portrait enhancement. Upload a dozen selfies, and it generates professional headshots in various styles. LinkedIn profiles across America have never looked better.

Quick Start
Turn your smartphone photos into professional marketing materials in under 10 minutes using *Canva*'s Magic Studio—upload your photo, use Magic Eraser to remove the background, then Magic Design to create multiple layout options automatically.

Video creation without film school

Runway pushes the boundaries of what's possible. Its Gen-2 feature creates video clips from text descriptions, while Magic Tools remove objects from existing footage with Hollywood-level precision. Indie filmmakers use it to achieve effects that previously required massive budgets.

Pictory specializes in turning long-form content into engaging short videos. Upload a blog post or article, and it automatically creates a video summary with relevant stock footage, captions, and transitions. Content creators use it to repurpose written content for social media.

Synthesia creates videos with AI-generated presenters. Choose from dozens of realistic avatars, type your script, and watch as your virtual spokesperson delivers your message in over 120 languages. Corporate training departments have embraced it for creating consistent, professional presentations.

Audio and voice specialists

The audio AI landscape has exploded with tools that make professional sound accessible to everyone. These specialized platforms understand the nuances of speech, music, and sound design in ways that general-purpose AI cannot match.

Did You Know?
While no AI-generated song has yet hit the Billboard Hot 100, "A Million Colors" became the first known AI-generated track to chart on TikTok's Viral 50, and "BBL Drizzy" became the first AI-generated song to receive official sample clearance when used in a charting track.

Voice generation and cloning

ElevenLabs leads voice cloning technology. Upload 30 seconds of someone reading, and it creates a digital voice that can say anything in that person's style. Audiobook narrators use it to maintain consistency across long projects, while podcasters create intro segments without scheduling studio time.

Murf takes a different approach with its library of professional AI voices. Choose from hundreds of options—different ages, accents, and speaking styles—then type your script. The results sound natural enough for commercials and presentations.

Speechify excels at converting text to speech for learning and accessibility. Its mobile app reads articles, emails, and documents aloud with remarkably human-like intonation. Students with dyslexia and busy commuters have made it a daily essential.

Music creation gets democratized

Udio and ***Suno*** have revolutionized music creation. Both platforms generate complete songs from text prompts—describe the mood, genre, and theme, and they compose original tracks with vocals, instruments, and professional mixing. Independent creators use them for podcast intros, YouTube background music, and even complete albums.

AIVA focuses specifically on classical and cinematic compositions. Film students and indie game developers rely on it for orchestral scores that would otherwise require hiring entire ensembles.

Did You Know?
AI-generated music is now eligible for streaming royalties on YouTube, Spotify, and Apple Music, creating new income opportunities for creators who combine AI composition with human arrangement.

Podcast production simplified

Descript combines transcription, editing, and AI enhancement in one platform. Upload raw audio, and it automatically removes "ums", adjusts pacing, and improves sound quality. The Overdub feature even lets you correct mistakes by typing new words—the AI generates them in your voice.

Adobe Podcast AI tackles the biggest amateur podcast problem: poor audio quality. Its Enhance Speech tool transforms recordings made in echo-filled rooms into studio-quality sound. The difference in sound quality is so dramatic that many people assume that it is too good to be true.

Hot Tip

Record a test sentence in your intended recording space, then run it through Adobe Podcast AI's enhancer. If the improvement is significant, you can skip expensive acoustic treatment and rely on AI post-processing instead.

Writing with a twist

While ***ChatGPT*** handles general writing tasks well, specialized AI writing tools excel in specific domains. These platforms understand industry conventions, audience expectations, and platform requirements that generic models often miss.

Next Level

Set up different AI writing assistants for different contexts—use *Grammarly GO* for professional emails, *Copy.ai* for marketing content, and *Sudowrite* for creative projects.

Marketing copy that converts

Copy.ai and ***Jasper*** dominate marketing copy creation. Both understand the psychology of sales writing, and generate headlines, email sequences, and ad copy that convert. *Copy.ai*'s *Brand Voice* feature learns your company's tone from existing content, ensuring consistency across campaigns.

Writesonic bridges general writing and marketing specialization. Its *Chatsonic* feature combines *ChatGPT*-style conversation with real-time web access and specialized templates for everything from product descriptions to press releases.

Creative writing gets AI assistance

Sudowrite has become the novelist's secret weapon. Unlike general AI that treats creative writing like any other text, *Sudowrite* understands story structure, character development, and pacing. Its Story Engine helps writers break through creative blocks by suggesting plot developments that fit their established narrative.

NovelCrafter takes world-building seriously. Upload character profiles, plot outlines, and setting details, and it maintains consistency across complex narratives. Fantasy and science fiction writers particularly appreciate how it tracks intricate details across multiple storylines.

NovelAI offers subscription-based creative writing with impressive customization. Writers can train it on their preferred styles and genres, creating a personalized writing assistant that understands their unique voice.

Professional communication enhanced

Grammarly GO extends beyond grammar checking into content generation. It understands context—an email to your boss gets different suggestions than a social media post. The AI adapts tone, formality, and style based on your intended audience.

Notion AI integrates seamlessly into existing workflows. Writers working within Notion databases can generate content that automatically follows their established templates and formatting. The AI understands project context and maintains consistency across documents.

Superhuman brings AI to email management. Its Smart Compose feature doesn't just complete sentences—it understands email patterns and suggests responses that match your communication style and your professional working relationships.

Hot Tip

AI writing tools work best when you give them your worst first draft, not a blank page. Write out your ideas roughly, then let AI refine style, structure, and clarity—it's faster and more authentic than starting from scratch.

Business power players

Enterprise AI tools tackle complex business challenges that consumer applications barely touch. These platforms understand industry workflows, data relationships, and professional requirements that generic AI models cannot handle effectively.

Data analysis made simple

Julius AI transforms data analysis from a specialist skill into an everyday capability. Upload spreadsheets, databases, or CSV files, and ask questions in plain English. "Which products had the highest growth last quarter?" gets answered with charts, trends, and actionable insights—no SQL knowledge required.

DataGPT takes business intelligence further by connecting to live data sources. Link your sales systems, marketing platforms, and customer databases, then ask complex questions like "Why did conversion rates drop in the Northeast region?". The AI investigates correlations and provides explanations backed by statistical analysis.

Polymer specializes in making complex datasets understandable. Its strength lies in automatic pattern recognition—upload your data, and it immediately identifies trends, outliers, and relationships you might have missed. Marketing teams use it to understand customer behavior patterns without requiring data science expertise.

Presentation creation revolutionized

Gamma has redefined slide creation. Describe your presentation topic and audience, and it generates complete slide decks with professional design, relevant content, and logical flow. Sales teams create pitch decks in minutes rather than hours.

Tome combines presentation creation with interactive storytelling. Its AI understands narrative structure and creates presentations that flow like compelling stories rather than bullet-point lists. Educators and trainers particularly appreciate how it maintains audience engagement.

Beautiful.AI focuses specifically on design excellence. While other tools generate content, *Beautiful.AI* ensures visual consistency and professional aesthetics. Every slide follows design principles automatically—no artistic training required.

Customer service automation

Intercom AI handles customer support conversations with remarkable sophistication. It understands context from previous interactions, accesses product databases, and escalates complex issues to human agents seamlessly. Customer satisfaction scores often improve because AI provides consistent, accurate responses 24/7.

Zendesk AI focuses on ticket management and resolution. It categorizes incoming requests, suggests responses based on similar past issues, and identifies customers likely to churn based on communication patterns. Support teams handle 40% more requests without adding staff.

Ada specializes in complex decision trees and troubleshooting. Its AI guides customers through multi-step problem resolution, accessing product manuals, warranty information, and installation guides. Technical support calls decrease significantly when customers can resolve issues independently.

Did You Know?

Small businesses using AI customer service tools see 40% faster response times and 25% higher customer satisfaction scores, primarily because AI never gets frustrated or tired during difficult conversations.

The creative playground

Creative AI tools have expanded beyond practical applications into pure experimentation and entertainment. These platforms encourage play, exploration, and artistic expression in ways that traditional software never could.

Interactive characters

Character.AI creates convincing conversations with historical figures, fictional characters, and specialized experts. Students practice language skills by chatting with native speakers, writers develop character voices by conversing with their creations, and history buffs debate with simulated historical figures.

Replika focuses on companionship and emotional connection. While controversial, many users report genuine benefits from having an AI friend who remembers conversations, provides emotional support, and offers judgment-free interaction. Mental health professionals are studying its potential therapeutic applications.

AI Dungeon transforms text-based gaming into unlimited creative storytelling. Players describe actions and scenarios while the AI generates responsive narratives that adapt to any plot direction. Game masters use it to create dynamic storylines that respond to player choices in real time.

Design and branding simplified

Looka democratizes logo design through AI understanding of visual psychology and brand principles. Answer questions about your business personality and target audience, and it generates dozens of logo concepts that feel professionally designed. Small businesses create brand identities without hiring design agencies.

Brandmark extends beyond logos into complete brand packages. It generates business cards, letterheads, social media templates, and brand guidelines that maintain visual consistency. Startups establish professional brand presence in hours rather than weeks.

Designs.ai offers an entire creative suite powered by AI. From logo creation to video editing to speech synthesis, it handles most visual communication needs under one subscription. Solo entrepreneurs particularly appreciate the all-in-one approach.

Social media mastery

Buffer AI transforms social media management from reactive posting to strategic content planning. It analyzes your audience engagement patterns, suggests optimal posting times, and generates content ideas that match your brand voice and audience interests.

Hootsuite Insights uses AI to analyze social media conversations and identify trending topics relevant to your industry. Marketing teams discover content opportunities and potential PR issues before they become major problems.

Later Influence focuses specifically on visual social media platforms. It analyzes your *Instagram* and *TikTok* performance, suggests hashtag strategies, and even predicts which types of content will perform best with your specific audience.

Next Level

Combine multiple creative AI tools for compound effects—use *Midjourney* to create base images, *Canva Magic Studio* to add text and branding, then *Buffer AI* to optimize posting strategy across platforms.

Tomorrow's contenders

The AI landscape evolves rapidly, with new tools launching weekly and existing platforms adding capabilities that blur traditional boundaries. Understanding emerging trends helps you stay ahead of the curve and discover tools before they become mainstream necessities.

Next-generation multi-modal AI

Google's Gemini represents the next generation of multi-modal AI. Unlike text-focused models, *Gemini* understands images, audio, video, and code simultaneously. Early users report impressive capabilities in analyzing complex documents that contain charts, diagrams, and mixed media content.

Microsoft Copilot variations are appearing across the entire *Office* ecosystem. *Excel Copilot* generates complex formulas from natural language requests, while *PowerPoint Copilot* creates presentations from simple outlines. The integration feels seamless because it understands how professionals actually work within these familiar tools.

Industry-specific innovations

Legal AI tools like ***Harvey*** and ***Casetext*** understand legal reasoning, case precedents, and regulatory requirements. Law firms use them for contract analysis, legal research, and brief writing—tasks that require specialized knowledge beyond general AI capabilities.

Medical AI platforms like ***Nuance DAX*** and ***Suki*** focus on clinical documentation and patient interaction analysis. Healthcare providers dictate patient encounters naturally, and the AI generates proper medical records that satisfy regulatory requirements and insurance documentation needs.

Education AI tools like ***Khanmigo*** and ***Socratic*** understand pedagogical principles and learning progression. They adapt explanations to individual student comprehension levels, and identify knowledge gaps that human teachers might miss in large classrooms.

What to watch for

Open-source alternatives are challenging commercial platforms across every category. ***Stable Diffusion*** proved that high-quality image generation doesn't require expensive subscriptions, and similar open-source projects are emerging for audio, video, and text generation.

Mobile-first AI tools recognize that most users interact with AI through smartphones. Apps like ***Luma AI*** create 3D models from phone videos, while ***Voicemod AI*** generates real-time voice effects during video calls. The future of AI is increasingly pocket-sized.

Platform integration is accelerating. Rather than standalone applications, AI capabilities are embedding directly into existing software. ***Adobe Creative Cloud***, ***Microsoft Office***, and ***Google Workspace*** are becoming AI-powered by default rather than offering separate AI tools.

Warning

Be cautious with AI tools that request extensive permissions or store sensitive data. Always review privacy policies and consider whether the convenience justifies sharing personal or business information.

Your next discovery

Choosing the right AI tool depends

on your specific needs rather than popular opinion. The best AI tool is the one that solves your immediate problem efficiently, not necessarily the one generating the most social media buzz.

If you create visual content regularly, start with ***Canva Magic Studio*** for its ease of use, then explore ***Midjourney*** for more artistic control.

If you work with audio or podcasts, ***Descript*** offers the most comprehensive solution for beginners and professionals alike.

If your business handles customer service, ***Intercom AI*** provides the most sophisticated conversation handling.

If you need data analysis, ***Julius AI*** translates complex questions into clear insights without requiring technical expertise.

If you write professionally, ***Copy.ai*** excels at marketing content while ***Sudowrite*** specializes in creative writing.

If you manage social media, ***Buffer AI*** combines content creation with strategic posting optimization.

Testing without commitment

Most AI tools offer free trials or freemium versions that provide genuine functionality rather than just demos. Start with free versions to understand capabilities and workflow integration before committing to subscriptions.

"The best AI tool is the one that solves your specific problem today, not the one everyone's talking about."

Create a simple test project that represents your typical use case. Rather than exploring every feature, focus on whether the tool solves your specific problem efficiently. Time yourself completing the same task manually versus with AI assistance—the time savings should be obvious and significant.

Building your personal AI toolkit

Successful AI adoption happens gradually rather than through wholesale replacement of existing workflows. Start with one tool that addresses your biggest pain point, master its core features, then gradually add complementary tools.

Focus on tools that integrate well together rather than collecting isolated solutions. ***Notion AI*** works seamlessly with existing *Notion* workflows, while ***Adobe AI*** features enhance familiar ***Photoshop*** and ***Illustrator*** projects. Integration reduces learning curves and increases adoption likelihood.

Consider subscription costs holistically rather than individually. Three separate $10 monthly subscriptions might be more expensive than one $25 comprehensive platform that handles multiple needs. Calculate total cost of ownership, including time spent learning and switching between tools.

Track your actual usage for the first month. Many users subscribe to multiple AI tools but regularly use only one or two. Honest usage tracking prevents subscription bloat and helps identify which tools truly add value to your workflow.

Quick Start

Choose one task you do weekly that takes more than 30 minutes, then test three different AI tools for that specific task. The winner becomes your gateway into AI-powered productivity.

Your AI toolkit should evolve with your needs and the rapidly changing technology landscape. The tools dominating today might be yesterday's news in six months, but the skills you develop in prompting, workflow integration, and AI-assisted thinking will remain valuable regardless of which specific platforms you use.

The future belongs to people who combine human creativity and judgment with AI capabilities. These specialized tools are your entry point into that future—choose wisely, experiment freely, and remember that the goal is augmenting your abilities rather than replacing your expertise. ■

Spotlight

Meet the people whose lives have been transformed (or at least nudged) by AI.

AI at work– supercharge your emails and meetings

Picture this: you arrive at work to find 47 emails waiting in your inbox–three of them marked "urgent"–and a calendar packed with back-to-back meetings. By 10 AM, you're already behind, drowning in a sea of unread messages and half-remembered action items from yesterday's project review.

Now, imagine walking out of that same 90-minute project meeting with perfect notes, every decision clearly documented, and action items automatically assigned with deadlines. Your email inbox shows you exactly which messages need immediate attention, and AI has already drafted thoughtful replies in your voice. This isn't science fiction—it's just another morning at the office with AI doing the administrative heavy lifting so that you can focus on actual work.

Your email inbox just got smarter

Email AI isn't about robots writing your messages—it's about having a super-smart assistant who reads everything, understands context, and helps you respond like the professional you are. Think of it as having someone who knows your communication style, remembers every conversation thread, and can spot the difference between "urgent" emails that can wait and genuine emergencies that need immediate attention.

Modern email AI works by analyzing patterns in your writing, understanding relationships between senders, and tracking the context of ongoing conversations. It learns that emails from your boss usually require quick responses, that marketing newsletters can wait, and that anything with "budget approval" in the subject line probably needs your immediate attention.

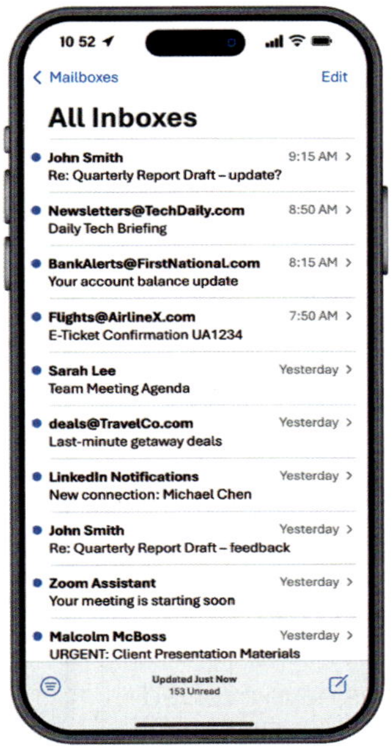

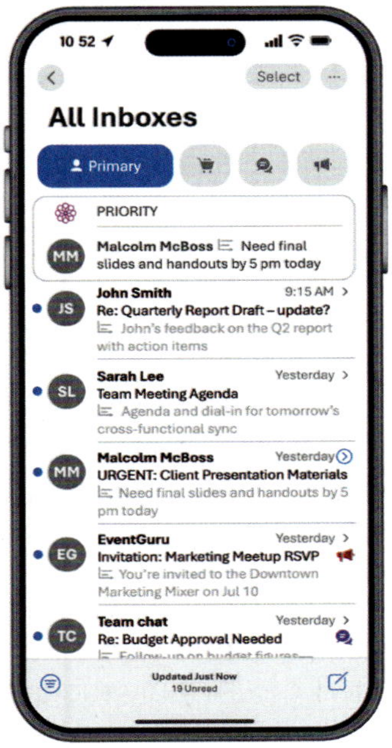

Did You Know?

Gmail's AI processes over 15 billion emails daily to improve its smart features, learning from patterns while keeping your personal data private.

Smart summaries that actually help

Long email threads with dozens of replies used to mean scrolling through a maze of quoted text, trying to piece together what actually happened. AI email tools now read these conversations like a seasoned project manager, extracting essential information and presenting it in digestible chunks.

Quick Start

Enable AI summaries in Gmail by clicking the sparkle icon next to long email threads—you'll get key points in seconds.

Gmail's Smart Compose and Smart Reply features automatically appear on threads with more than three messages, highlighting decisions made, questions asked, and action items mentioned. Microsoft Outlook's Copilot goes a step further, identifying when someone changes their position on an issue or when new stakeholders join the conversation.

The real magic happens with priority detection. AI learns that emails from certain people always need quick responses, that anything mentioning "deadline" or "approval" should rise to the top, and that newsletters from industry publications can wait until Friday afternoon. Your most important messages get flagged automatically, while routine

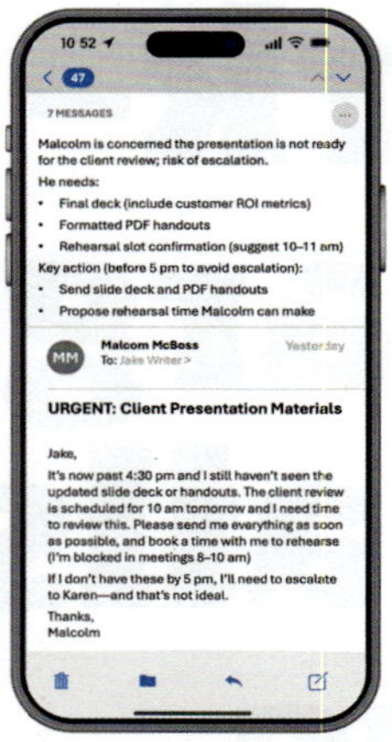

notifications stay quietly organized for later review.

Hot Tip

Train your email AI by manually marking emails as important or unimportant for the first week—it learns your priorities faster than waiting for pattern recognition.

Platform differences matter. Apple Mail's Intelligent Tracking Protection focuses on privacy while offering basic smart features. Gmail's AI integration runs deeper, offering Smart Compose suggestions that complete entire sentences. Outlook's Copilot excels at business context, understanding corporate hierarchies and project timelines better than consumer-focused alternatives.

1. Click the **Settings** gear icon
2. Select the **General** tab
3. Scroll to **Smart features**
4. Enable **Smart Compose** and **Smart Reply**
5. Choose **Writing suggestions** level

Reply suggestions that sound like you

AI reply suggestions have evolved far beyond the generic "Thanks for your email" responses. Modern systems analyze your writing patterns, preferred phrases, and typical response styles to generate replies that actually sound like they came from you.

The technology works by studying your email history—how you typically greet colleagues versus external contacts, whether you prefer formal or casual language, and how you usually phrase requests or confirmations. After a few weeks of learning, AI can draft responses that match your voice so well that recipients won't know you had help.

Warning

Always review AI-generated replies before sending, especially for sensitive topics or important business communications.

Smart email AI also adjusts tone based on context. It suggests more formal language for client communications, casual responses for team members, and appropriately diplomatic phrasing for sensitive situations. The system recognizes when someone is frustrated or when a situation requires extra tact, adjusting its suggestions accordingly.

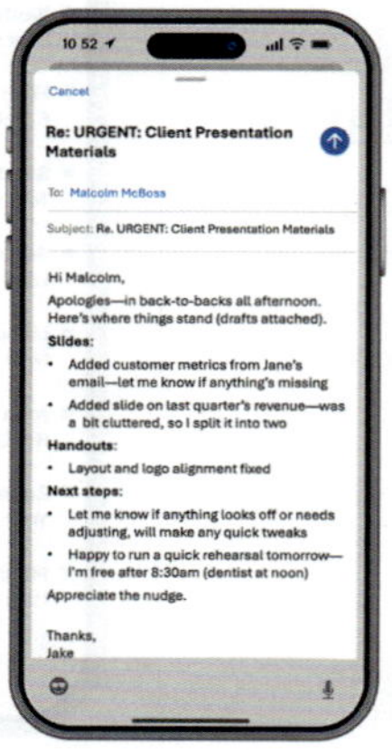

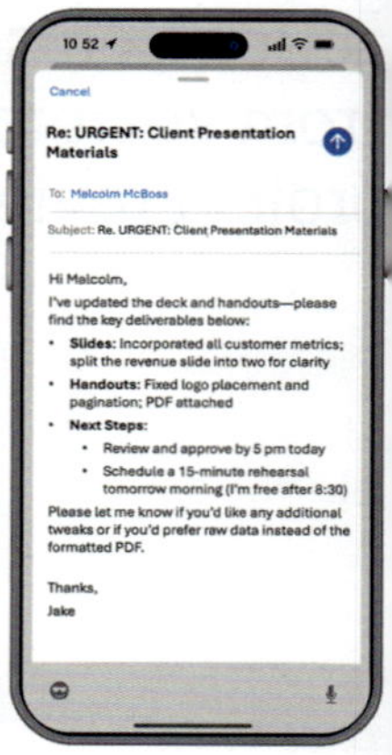

Next Level

Set up email templates for common responses, then let AI customize them based on the specific situation—this saves time while maintaining personalization.

The learning process varies by platform. Gmail's Smart AI typically needs 2-3 weeks of regular use to understand your style. Outlook's Copilot can import writing samples from other Microsoft apps to accelerate learning. Third-party tools like Grammarly and Jasper offer more aggressive AI assistance but require separate subscriptions.

Meetings that don't waste your time

The average knowledge worker spends more than 20 hours per week in meetings, yet most people leave those sessions with incomplete notes and unclear action items. AI meeting tools transform passive note-taking into active participation by handling documentation automatically, letting you focus on contributing to discussions rather than frantically scribbling notes.

Modern meeting AI goes beyond simple transcription. It understands the difference between casual conversation and important decisions, recognizes when someone is assigning a task versus making a suggestion, and can even identify when discussions go off-topic or when key people haven't weighed in on important points.

Did You Know?

AI meeting tools can achieve higher than 90% accuracy in transcription—even with multiple speakers, background noise, and technical jargon—better than most human note-takers.

Real-time transcription and smart notes

AI transcription tools like Otter.ai, Microsoft Teams Premium, or Zoom's AI Companion don't just convert speech to text—they understand context, identify speakers, and organize information by topic. They recognize technical terms specific to your industry, correctly spell proper names after hearing them once, and can even handle multiple people talking simultaneously.

The real breakthrough comes with intelligent organization. Instead of producing a wall of text, AI meeting tools create structured notes with clear sections for decisions made, action items assigned, questions raised, and follow-up topics. They can identify when someone commits to a deadline, when a decision gets overturned, or when important information gets mentioned in passing.

Smart meeting AI also recognizes patterns in your organization's communication style. It learns that when your CEO says "let's circle back on this" it usually means the topic is tabled, or that when the project manager asks "Who can own this?" they're looking for specific task assignments.

Did You Know?

AI meeting tools can identify key moments even in 3-hour sessions, creating summaries that highlight just the 10 minutes of decisions that actually matter.

Platform capabilities differ significantly. Zoom's AI Companion excels at identifying action items and creating summaries. Microsoft Teams Premium integrates seamlessly with other Office apps, automatically adding action items to Planner or To Do. Google Meet's AI features work best with

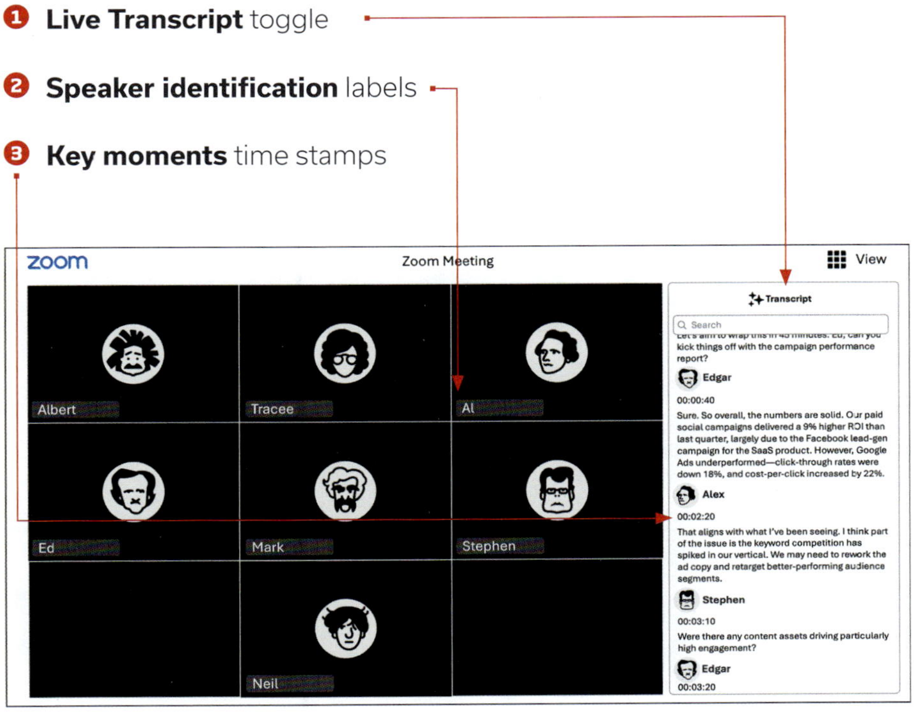

Google Workspace accounts, and can schedule follow-up meetings based on discussion points.

Follow-up that follows through

The best meeting AI tools don't stop when the call ends—they automatically generate summaries, extract action items with assigned owners, and can even draft follow-up emails. This automation ensures nothing falls through the cracks and gives everyone a shared understanding of what was decided.

Advanced systems like Microsoft Copilot or Google Meet's AI features can identify when someone volunteers for a task, recognize deadline commitments, and flag when important questions go unanswered. They create different output formats for different audiences—detailed notes for project files, executive summaries for leadership, and personalized action lists for individual team members.

Next Level

Set up automatic calendar blocking for action items mentioned in meetings—AI can suggest time slots based on mentioned deadlines and your availability.

The follow-through automation extends to task management systems. AI can automatically create tickets in Jira, add items to Asana boards, or update project status in Monday.com based on meeting discussions. This integration means decisions made in meetings immediately become trackable work items.

Integration capabilities vary by platform. Microsoft's ecosystem offers the deepest integration, connecting Teams, Outlook, Planner, and Project automatically. Google Workspace provides solid integration within its own apps but its integration is limited with third-party connections. Zoom offers strong integration with popular project management tools through Zapier and direct API connections.

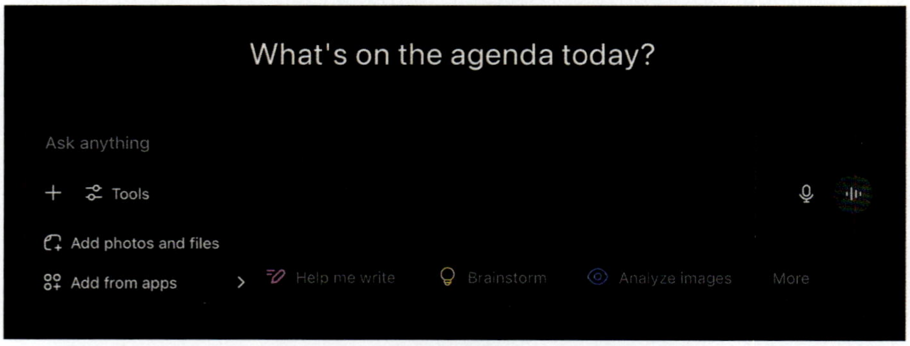

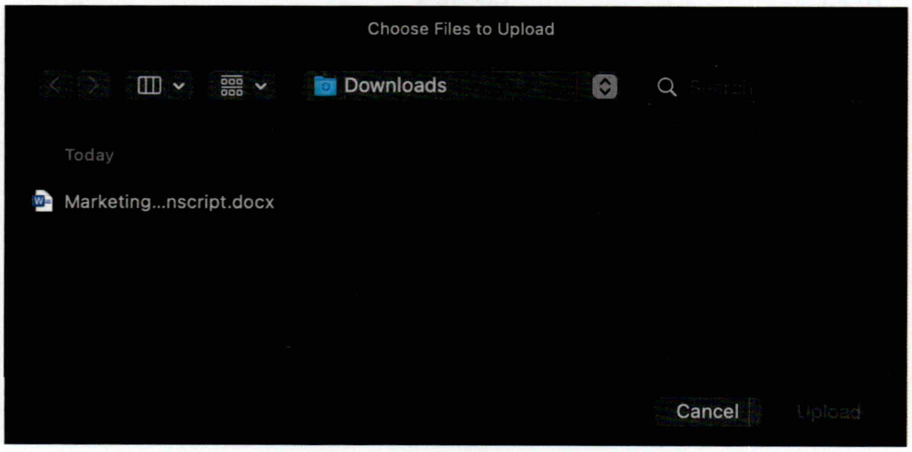

Warning

Double-check AI-generated action items before sharing—sometimes AI misinterprets casual comments as formal commitments.

Project: turn meeting chaos into clear action

Let's walk through transforming a messy 45-minute team meeting into organized, actionable documentation. We'll use a realistic scenario—a monthly marketing review where multiple topics get discussed, decisions change mid-conversation, and several action items emerge from side discussions.

Your Mission: Take a typical meeting transcript (the kind where people talk over each other, go off on tangents, and circle back to previous topics) and create three outputs: an executive summary for leadership, a detailed action plan for the team, and follow-up emails for stakeholders who missed the meeting.

1. **Upload Your Transcript:** Most AI tools accept audio files, video recordings, or text transcripts. For this project, you can use a real recording from Zoom, Teams, or Google Meet, or work with a transcript

if privacy policies require it. Upload the file to your chosen AI tool—ChatGPT, Claude, or Perplexity all handle long-form content well

Quick Start

If you don't have a real meeting transcript, use this prompt to generate a realistic example: "Create a 45-minute marketing team meeting transcript with 4 participants discussing campaign performance, budget reallocation, and Q4 planning".

2 **Craft Your Analysis Prompt:** Don't just ask for a summary—be specific about what you need. Try the RTF (Role, Task, Format) framework: "Role: You're an assistant to a busy leadership team, skilled at spotting key decisions and next steps; Task: Analyze this meeting transcript and produce three deliverables; Format: (1) Executive Summary—a 2-paragraph overview highlighting key decisions and their business impact; (2) Action Plan—a table listing each action with its owner and due date; (3) Follow-Up Email—a polished message to stakeholders who missed the meeting"

3 **Extract Action Items with Precision:** Ask the AI to identify not just what needs to be done, but who committed to doing it and when. Use this follow-up prompt: "Create a table showing each action item, the person responsible, the deadline mentioned or implied, and any dependencies on other tasks or team members"

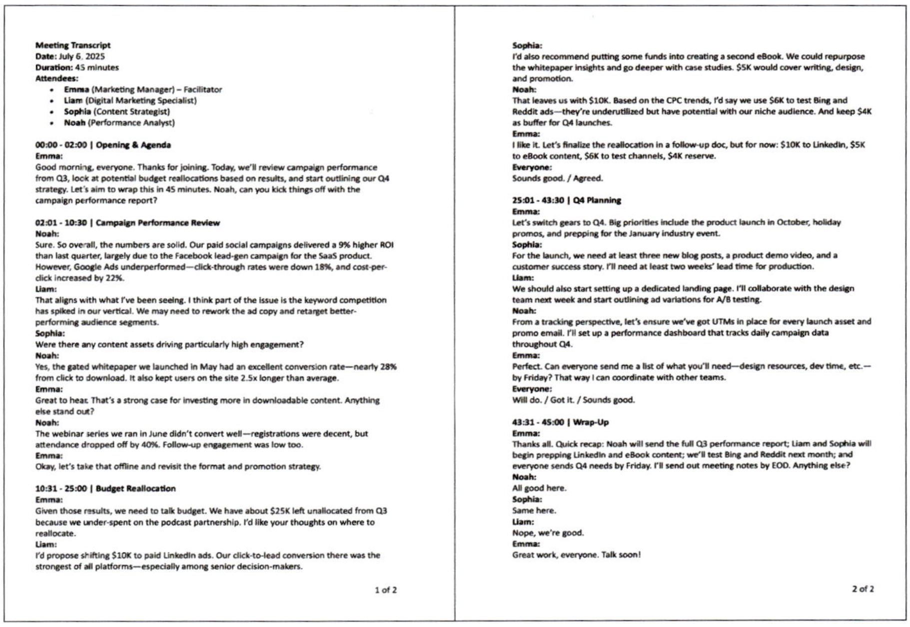

Meeting Transcript
Date: July 6, 2025
Duration: 45 minutes
Attendees:

- **Emma** (Marketing Manager) – Facilitator
- **Liam** (Digital Marketing Specialist)
- **Sophia** (Content Strategist)
- **Noah** (Performance Analyst)

00:00 - 02:00 | Opening & Agenda
Emma:
Good morning, everyone. Thanks for joining. Today, we'll review campaign performance from Q3, look at potential budget reallocations based on results, and start outlining our Q4 strategy. Let's aim to wrap this in 45 minutes. Noah, can you kick things off with the campaign performance report?

02:01 - 10:30 | Campaign Performance Review
Noah:
Sure. So overall, the numbers are solid. Our paid social campaigns delivered a 9% higher ROI than last quarter, largely due to the Facebook lead-gen campaign for the SaaS product. However, Google Ads underperformed—click-through rates were down 18%, and cost-per-click increased by 22%.
Liam:
That aligns with what I've been seeing. I think part of the issue is the keyword competition has spiked in our vertical. We may need to rework the ad copy and retarget better-performing audience segments.
Sophia:
Were there any content assets driving particularly high engagement?
Noah:
Yes, the gated whitepaper we launched in May had an excellent conversion rate—nearly 28% from click to download. It also kept users on the site 2.5x longer than average.
Emma:
Great to hear. That's a strong case for investing more in downloadable content. Anything else stand out?
Noah:
The webinar series we ran in June didn't convert well—registrations were decent, but attendance dropped off by 40%. Follow-up engagement was low too.
Emma:
Okay, let's take that offline and revisit the format and promotion strategy.

10:31 - 25:00 | Budget Reallocation
Emma:
Given those results, we need to talk budget. We have about $25K left unallocated from Q3 because we under-spent on the podcast partnership. I'd like your thoughts on where to reallocate.
Liam:
I'd propose shifting $10K to paid LinkedIn ads. Our click-to-lead conversion there was the strongest of all platforms—especially among senior decision-makers.

1 of 2

Sophia:
I'd also recommend putting some funds into creating a second eBook. We could repurpose the whitepaper insights and go deeper with case studies. $5K would cover writing, design, and promotion.
Noah:
That leaves us with $10K. Based on the CPC trends, I'd say we use $6K to test Bing and Reddit ads—they're underutilized but have potential with our niche audience. And keep $4K as buffer for Q4 launches.
Emma:
I like it. Let's finalize the reallocation in a follow-up doc, but for now: $10K to LinkedIn, $5K to eBook content, $6K to test channels, $4K reserve.
Everyone:
Sounds good. / Agreed.

25:01 - 43:30 | Q4 Planning
Emma:
Let's switch gears to Q4. Big priorities include the product launch in October, holiday promos, and prepping for the January industry event.
Sophia:
For the launch, we need at least three new blog posts, a product demo video, and a customer success story. I'll need at least two weeks' lead time for production.
Liam:
We should also start setting up a dedicated landing page. I'll collaborate with the design team next week and start outlining ad variations for A/B testing.
Noah:
From a tracking perspective, let's ensure we've got UTMs in place for every launch asset and promo email. I'll set up a performance dashboard that tracks daily campaign data throughout Q4.
Emma:
Perfect. Can everyone send me a list of what you'll need—design resources, dev time, etc.—by Friday? That way I can coordinate with other teams.
Everyone:
Will do. / Got it. / Sounds good.

43:31 - 45:00 | Wrap-Up
Emma:
Thanks all. Quick recap: Noah will send the full Q3 performance report; Liam and Sophia will begin prepping LinkedIn and eBook content; we'll test Bing and Reddit next month; and everyone sends Q4 needs by Friday. I'll send out meeting notes by EOD. Anything else?
Noah:
All good here.
Sophia:
Same here.
Liam:
Nope, we're good.
Emma:
Great work, everyone. Talk soon!

2 of 2

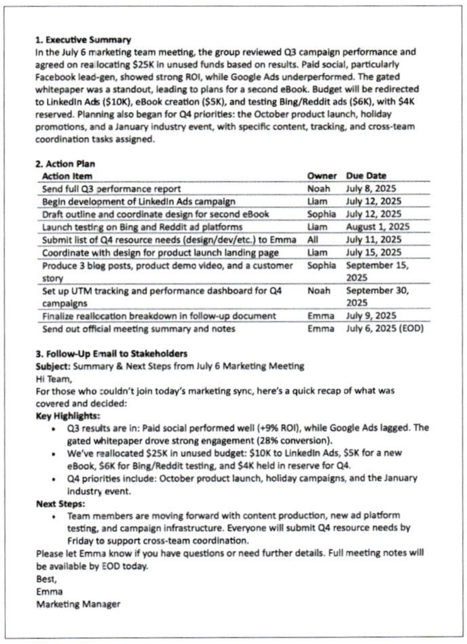

1. Executive Summary
In the July 6 marketing team meeting, the group reviewed Q3 campaign performance and agreed on reallocating $25K in unused funds based on results. Paid social, particularly Facebook lead-gen, showed strong ROI, while Google Ads underperformed. The gated whitepaper was a standout, leading to plans for a second eBook. Budget will be redirected to LinkedIn Ads ($10K), eBook creation ($5K), and testing Bing/Reddit ads ($6K), with $4K reserved. Planning also began for Q4 priorities: the October product launch, holiday promotions, and a January industry event, with specific content, tracking, and cross-team coordination tasks assigned.

2. Action Plan

Action Item	Owner	Due Date
Send full Q3 performance report	Noah	July 8, 2025
Begin development of LinkedIn Ads campaign	Liam	July 12, 2025
Draft outline and coordinate design for second eBook	Sophia	July 12, 2025
Launch testing on Bing and Reddit ad platforms	Liam	August 1, 2025
Submit list of Q4 resource needs (design/dev/etc.) to Emma	All	July 11, 2025
Coordinate with design for product launch landing page	Liam	July 15, 2025
Produce 3 blog posts, product demo video, and a customer story	Sophia	September 15, 2025
Set up UTM tracking and performance dashboard for Q4 campaigns	Noah	September 30, 2025
Finalize reallocation breakdown in follow-up document	Emma	July 9, 2025
Send out official meeting summary and notes	Emma	July 6, 2025 (EOD)

3. Follow-Up Email to Stakeholders
Subject: Summary & Next Steps from July 6 Marketing Meeting
Hi Team,
For those who couldn't join today's marketing sync, here's a quick recap of what was covered and decided:
Key Highlights:

- Q3 results are in: Paid social performed well (+9% ROI), while Google Ads lagged. The gated whitepaper drove strong engagement (28% conversion).
- We've reallocated $25K in unused budget: $10K to LinkedIn Ads, $5K for a new eBook, $6K for Bing/Reddit testing, and $4K held in reserve for Q4.
- Q4 priorities include: October product launch, holiday campaigns, and the January industry event.

Next Steps:

- Team members are moving forward with content production, new ad platform testing, and campaign infrastructure. Everyone will submit Q4 resource needs by Friday to support cross-team coordination.

Please let Emma know if you have questions or need further details. Full meeting notes will be available by EOD today.
Best,
Emma
Marketing Manager

4 **Generate Multiple Output Formats:** The same meeting information serves different audiences. Ask for: "Reformat these findings as (1) Bullet points for project management software, (2) A narrative summary for the project file, (3) Individual task lists for each team member mentioned"

5 **Refine and Personalize:** AI outputs are starting points, not finished products. Review the generated content for accuracy, adjust the tone to match your organization's communication style, and add any context the AI might have missed. Pay special attention to deadlines—AI sometimes interprets "next week" in a different way to humans

Hot Tip

Save successful prompt templates for future meetings—once you find phrasing that works well with your team's communication style, reuse it for consistency.

The transformation is dramatic. What started as 45 minutes of scattered conversation becomes a clear roadmap with specific accountability. Team members know exactly what they committed to, leadership understands the key decisions, and everyone has documentation they can reference weeks later.

Making it work in your workplace

Implementing AI meeting and email tools in most organizations requires more diplomacy than technical skill. The biggest hurdles aren't technological—they're cultural and procedural. Success comes from demonstrating value before asking for permission and addressing concerns about privacy and job security upfront.

The key is starting small with tools that don't require IT approval or budget sign-offs. Browser-based AI tools and personal subscriptions let you prove the concept before proposing enterprise-wide adoption.

Did You Know?

Over 70% of successful workplace AI implementations start with individual adoption before expanding to team- or company-wide use.

Getting started without IT approval

Most effective workplace AI tools work through web browsers or as plugins that don't require software installation. Gmail's AI features activate automatically for Google Workspace accounts. Otter.ai connects to Zoom, Teams, and Google Meet without administrator permissions. ChatGPT and Claude handle meeting transcripts through simple copy-and-paste.

Warning

Never upload confidential client information or proprietary data to public AI tools—use Enterprise versions or on-premises solutions for sensitive content.

Start with your own meetings and email workflow. Use AI tools for internal team discussions before expanding to client communications. Document your time savings and improved follow-through, creating a compelling case study for broader adoption.

Privacy considerations vary by organization and industry. Financial services, healthcare, and legal firms often require Enterprise AI solutions with specific data-handling guarantees. Tech companies and startups typically have more flexibility with cloud-based tools. Know your organization's data policies before uploading meeting recordings or email content.

Quick Start

Begin with one week of using AI for internal team emails only—track time saved and accuracy improvements to build your business case.

The compliance landscape in the US differs by industry:

Healthcare: Requires HIPAA-compliant AI tools like Microsoft's Healthcare Bot or AWS HealthLake.

Finance: Needs SOX-compliant solutions like IBM Watson or enterprise Microsoft 365.

Legal: Demands attorney-client privilege protection through tools like LegalMation or Ross Intelligence.

Education: Requires FERPA compliance, often met by Google Workspace for Education or Microsoft Education.

Government: Needs FedRAMP authorization, available through AWS GovCloud or Microsoft Government.

Other countries have their own compliance standards.

Building team buy-in

Resistance to AI tools usually stems from fear of replacement rather than technical concerns. Frame AI as augmentation, not automation. Show colleagues how AI frees them from administrative tasks so that they can focus on creative problem-solving and relationship building.

Share concrete results that matter to your team. Instead of talking about AI capabilities, show how it helped you respond to client emails 30% faster or how meeting summaries prevented three separate "Wait, what did we decide?" follow-up conversations.

Next Level

Become the team's AI champion by offering to handle meeting summaries for important sessions—colleagues will quickly see the value when they receive clear, actionable notes.

Address concerns directly. Acknowledge that AI tools aren't perfect and need human oversight. Explain how AI learning works—that these systems improve with feedback rather than replace human judgment. Share examples of AI mistakes you've caught and corrected, demonstrating the human-AI collaboration model.

Hot Tip

Create a shared document with AI prompts that work well for your team's specific needs—democratize the learning process and build collective expertise.

The most successful workplace AI adoption happens when early adopters become internal advocates, sharing their positive experiences and helping colleagues overcome initial hesitation. Track specific metrics: average email response time, meeting follow-up completion rates, and team satisfaction with documentation quality.

Troubleshooting common problems

Even the best AI tools occasionally misunderstand context or produce unhelpful outputs. Knowing how to troubleshoot these issues prevents frustration and maintains team confidence in AI assistance.

- **Email AI suggests inappropriate tone:** This usually happens when the AI hasn't learned your communication style yet. Manually edit suggested replies for the first two weeks, and the AI will adapt to your preferred tone and formality level.
- **Meeting AI misses important decisions:** Check that your audio quality is clear and speakers are close to microphones. AI performs better with single speakers than overlapping conversations. For complex discussions, pause periodically to summarize key points aloud.
- **Action items assigned to wrong people:** AI sometimes confuses pronouns or indirect references. Train it by explicitly stating "John will handle this" rather than "he'll take care of it" when making assignments.

Warning

AI tools struggle with sarcasm, jokes, and cultural references—review outputs carefully when these elements appear in meetings or emails.

- **Transcription accuracy drops with technical terms:** Upload glossaries of industry-specific terms, product names, and employee names to your AI tools. Most platforms allow custom vocabulary that improves recognition accuracy.
- **Privacy concerns from team members:** Address these by demonstrating data-handling policies, showing how to delete transcripts after processing, and offering alternatives like on-device AI tools for sensitive discussions.

Your productivity upgrade starts now

The best time to start using AI for email and meetings is right now, with your next inbox review or upcoming team call. Choose one area—either email management or meeting documentation—and commit to using AI tools consistently for one week.

For email, enable AI features in your current email client or try a browser extension that adds smart summaries and reply suggestions. For meetings, start recording sessions (with permission) and using AI for transcription and action-item extraction.

Quick Start

This week's goal—use AI to handle meeting notes for three different sessions, and track how much time you save on post-meeting follow-up.

Track specific metrics that matter: time saved on email processing, accuracy of meeting action items, and team feedback on documentation quality. Most people see 25-40% time savings on administrative tasks within the first month.

The productivity gains compound over time. Week one shows basic time savings. Week three reveals improved accuracy and consistency. By week six, you'll notice better team communication and fewer missed deadlines because everyone has clear, actionable documentation.

Did You Know?

Organizations using AI for meetings and email report significantly fewer "What did we decide?" follow-up conversations and much higher action-item completion rates.

Your productivity upgrade isn't about working faster—it's about working smarter, focusing your energy on high-value activities while AI handles the routine tasks that used to consume hours of your day.

Remember the ROI calculation: if you save 90 minutes per week on email and meeting administration, that's 78 hours annually—nearly two full work weeks you can redirect to strategic thinking, relationship building, and creative problem-solving. ■

AI for family–share the load and stay connected

Picture this: It's Monday morning. Soccer cleats are missing, permission slips need signatures, someone forgot lunch money, and three kids need to be in different places at the same time. Meanwhile, your spouse texts that they're stuck in traffic and can't make pick-up. Sound familiar?

What if I told you that AI can transform this daily chaos into smooth-running family coordination? We're not talking about robots doing your parenting—we're talking about smart tools that handle the mental load so that you can focus on what matters most: actually spending time with your family.

Your family's new digital command center

Gone are the days when family coordination meant a giant wall calendar covered in different-colored pens. Today's AI-powered family management systems work like having a personal assistant who never sleeps, never forgets, and never gets overwhelmed by conflicting schedules.

Smart calendar integration that actually works

The magic starts when your family calendars stop being separate islands of information. AI calendar tools like ***Google Calendar***'s smart scheduling or ***Calendly***'s family features automatically detect scheduling

conflicts before they become problems. When your daughter's soccer game gets moved and now conflicts with your son's piano recital, you'll get an alert with suggested solutions—not just a notification that your day just got impossible.

These systems learn your family's patterns. They know that soccer practice means leaving 20 minutes early because of traffic conditions. They remember that Tuesday nights are homework nights. They even factor in travel time between locations automatically.

Essential family calendar features include:

- Automatic travel-time calculations
- Conflict-detection alerts
- Multi-person scheduling
- Cross-platform synchronization

1. Overlapping events highlighted
2. Suggested resolution options
3. Automatic travel-time calculations
4. Family member color coding
5. Shared event notifications

Task assignment that sticks

Traditional chore charts fail because they're static. AI-powered task management adapts to real life. ***Todoist*** and ***Any.do*** now offer family features that reassign tasks when someone gets sick or has a school event. The system learns who's good at what, and adjusts accordingly.

Your teenager didn't take out the trash? The system automatically reassigns it and adjusts their other responsibilities. No nagging required—just smooth redistribution that keeps the household running.

Notification systems that don't overwhelm

The key difference between helpful AI and annoying spam lies in smart notifications. Modern family management AI learns when you need reminders and when you don't. It sends one gentle nudge, not seventeen panic alerts.

Hot Tip

Link family calendars to location services—get automatic travel-time alerts that actually account for current traffic conditions.

These systems understand context. A reminder about tomorrow's early soccer practice gets sent Sunday evening, not at midnight. Grocery list updates appear when you're actually near a store, not when you're in a meeting.

Meal planning without the mental load

The daily "What's for dinner?" question creates more stress than most families realize. AI meal planning tools eliminate this decision fatigue by learning your family's preferences, dietary restrictions, and schedule constraints.

Smart grocery lists that build themselves

PlateJoy and ***Mealime*** generate meal plans based on your family's eating patterns, then automatically create shopping lists organized by store layout. These aren't generic meal plans—they're personalized to your kids' preferences, your cooking skill level, and how much time you actually have on busy weeknights.

The AI remembers that your youngest won't eat anything green except broccoli, that Thursday nights need 30-minute meals because of late practices, and that you prefer batch cooking on Sundays. It builds meal plans that work with your real life, not against it.

Dietary considerations AI handles seamlessly:

- Vegetarian/vegan preferences
- Allergy restrictions
- Heart-healthy options
- Kid-friendly modifications
- Time-constrained meal prep

Meal planning based on family preferences and schedules

Advanced meal planning AI considers your calendar when suggesting recipes. It knows to recommend crockpot meals on days with evening activities, and suggests quick breakfast options before early morning games. Some systems even adjust portion sizes based on who's eating at home each night.

Pepperplate and ***BigOven*** integrate with your calendar to suggest meals that match your schedule. Late soccer practice tonight? You'll get slow cooker recipes that finish when you get home. Early Saturday game? Overnight oats suggestions appear automatically.

The AI learns seasonal preferences too. It suggests heartier soups during winter months, and lighter salads when temperatures rise. Holiday planning becomes effortless when the system automatically suggests traditional family favorites and accommodates visiting relatives.

Inventory management that prevents food waste

Smart pantry management might sound futuristic, but it's surprisingly practical. Apps like ***FoodNanny*** and ***StillTasty*** track expiration dates and suggest recipes using ingredients you already have. Some families save $100-200 monthly just by reducing food waste.

Did You Know?

AI meal planners can reduce food waste by up to 30% while cutting grocery costs by an average of $150 monthly for families of four.

The AI learns your shopping patterns and warns you before buying duplicates. It suggests using that second jar of pasta sauce you forgot about, and creates leftover transformation recipes that actually appeal to your family.

Managing the kid activity circus

Modern family life often feels like a complex logistics operation. Soccer, piano, tutoring, playdates, birthday parties—keeping track of who needs to be where (and when) challenges even the most organized parents.

Automated schedule conflict detection

AI scheduling tools examine your entire family's commitments and flag conflicts before they blindside you. ***Cozi*** and ***FamCal*** analyze travel times, preparation needs, and overlapping commitments to alert you to potential problems days in advance.

The system doesn't just tell you about conflicts—it suggests solutions. When Saturday's soccer tournament conflicts with a birthday party, it might recommend asking another parent for a ride, or suggest arriving late to the party after the game ends.

Carpool coordination made simple

Carpool management becomes exponentially easier with AI assistance. ***GoKid*** and similar platforms automatically match families with similar routes and schedules. The AI handles the complex calculations of fair distribution, and tracks who owes driving duties.

The system sends automatic reminders, handles weather cancellations, and even manages backup plans when regular drivers aren't available. Parents report saving 3-4 hours weekly on driving duties through smart carpool coordination.

Equipment and permission slip tracking

Nothing creates Monday morning panic like realizing soccer cleats are at school or permission slips are due today. AI-powered family apps create automated reminder systems that prevent these common disasters.

Warning

Always verify AI-generated schedules against official team and school communications—technology enhances human oversight, but doesn't replace it.

TeamSnap and ***LeagueApps*** send equipment reminders based on practice schedules and weather forecasts. They track permission slip deadlines and automatically remind you with enough lead time to avoid last-minute stress.

Weather-based notifications make game day preparation effortless. Rain forecasts trigger reminders for indoor gym shoes. Hot weather alerts suggest extra water bottles. Tournament weekends get special packing checklists that account for multiple games and varying conditions.

Seasonal schedule planning

AI excels at managing seasonal transitions that overwhelm traditional planning methods. When Fall sports overlap with back-to-school activities, the system anticipates conflicts and suggests schedule adjustments weeks in advance.

Tournament seasons require special coordination that AI handles smoothly. The system tracks multi-day events, hotel bookings, and complicated arrival times. It creates family travel plans that account for multiple children's different tournament schedules.

Holiday planning becomes stress-free when AI coordinates family traditions with activity schedules. The system remembers that Christmas Eve soccer practice conflicts with church services, and suggests alternatives that maintain both traditions.

Emergency planning and safety coordination

Family emergencies demand immediate coordination across multiple people and locations. AI-powered emergency planning ensures your family stays connected and informed when unexpected situations arise.

AI-powered emergency preparedness

Modern emergency planning goes beyond basic contact lists. ***Life360*** and ***Find My Family*** use AI to create comprehensive emergency response systems that adapt to your family's specific needs and locations.

These systems monitor weather alerts, school closures, and local emergencies to provide proactive notifications. When severe weather threatens your area, you'll get alerts with family-specific action plans rather than generic warnings.

The AI learns your family's routine locations and creates customized emergency meetup points. It considers work schedules, school locations, and typical family whereabouts to suggest realistic emergency plans that account for where everyone actually spends their time.

Family location tracking that respects privacy

Location sharing creates safety benefits while raising privacy concerns. AI-powered family location systems like ***Glympse*** and ***Life360*** provide safety oversight without constant surveillance.

The AI learns normal family patterns and only alerts when someone deviates significantly from expected routines. Your teenager's phone battery died at school? You'll get a notification. They stopped for ice cream on the way home? The system recognizes this as normal behavior and stays quiet.

Smart location systems distinguish between safety concerns and privacy boundaries. They provide enough information for emergency coordination while respecting individual autonomy as children mature.

Emergency planning app showing?

1. Family location status
2. Emergency contact cascade
3. Local alert integration
4. Meetup point suggestions
5. Emergency kit checklist

Medical information and emergency contacts

Medical emergencies require immediate access to critical health information. ***ICE (In Case of Emergency)*** apps use AI to organize medical data, insurance information, and emergency contacts in formats that first responders can access quickly.

The system maintains updated medication lists, allergy information, and medical condition details for each family member. When emergency situations arise, critical health information is immediately available to medical professionals.

Warning

Test family emergency protocols monthly—AI tools are only as good as the information you keep current.

Project: build your family activity roster

Let's tackle the biggest family coordination challenge: creating a weekly activity roster that actually works. This project transforms your weekly planning from reactive scrambling to proactive organization.

Your mission

Create an AI-generated family activity roster that includes pick-up and drop-off times, conflict alerts, carpool opportunities, and backup plans. You'll use either ***ChatGPT*** or ***Claude*** to build a comprehensive system that adapts to your family's specific needs.

Choosing your AI tool

For complex family scheduling, ***Claude*** excels at processing multiple variables and creating detailed organizational systems. ***ChatGPT*** works better for ongoing conversational refinement of your roster. Both can handle this project effectively.

Quick Start

Screenshot your current family calendar before starting—you'll be amazed at the before/after transformation.

The SPARK prompt template

Here's your power prompt for complex family scheduling, based on the SPARK framework:

Situation: For a family with [number] children aged [ages] with activities including [detailed list with times and locations].

Purpose: As a family organization expert specializing in activity logistics and time management for busy parents.

Action: Build a comprehensive weekly roster so that drop-offs/ pick-ups run smoothly.

Result: As a weekly grid with 7 daily entries, showing each child's activities with start time, drop-off/pick-up times, and note any potential overlaps or tight turnarounds.

Knowledge: Notes: [drive time], [parent availability], etc.

Example

"We're a family with three children: Emma (aged 12, has soccer on Tuesdays and Thursdays from 4-6 pm), Jake (aged 9, has piano on Wednesdays at 4:00 pm and basketball on Saturdays at 10 am), and Lily (aged 6, has swimming on Wednesdays at 4:30 pm). As a family organization expert specializing in activity logistics and time management for busy parents, build a comprehensive weekly roster so that drop-offs/ pick-ups run smoothly, as a weekly grid with 7 daily entries, showing each child's activities with start time, drop-off/pick-up times, and note any potential overlaps or tight turnarounds. Notes: Activities are across town, about 15-20 minutes' drive time apart. Both parents work until 5 pm weekdays."

❶ AI-generated structured weekly grid
❷ Departure times accounting for traffic patterns
❸ Conflict alerts

Refinement techniques

Your first AI-generated roster will be good, but follow-up prompts make it great:

"Add backup plans for when parents are stuck in meetings", "Include equipment checklists for each activity", "Suggest carpool coordination with [specific families]", "Factor in homework

🗓️ Weekly Family Activity Schedule (with Logistics) ❶

Day	Emma (12)	Jake (9)	Lily (6)	Notes / Logistics
Monday	— ❷	—	—	No scheduled activities. Consider homework/family dinner.
Tuesday	**Soccer: 4–6pm** 🕓 Drop-off: 3:40pm 🕕 Pickup: 6:00pm	—	—	❸ ⚠ Parent working until 5pm → need after-school sitter or help for 3:40pm drop-off.
Wednesday	—	**Piano: 4:00pm** 🕓 Drop-off: 3:40pm 🕓 Pickup: 4:30pm	**Swimming: 4:30pm** 🕓 Drop-off: 4:10pm 🕔 Pickup: 5:00pm	⚠ Overlap: Jake's pickup = Lily's drop-off. Need 2nd driver or help. 🕔 Parents available for final pickups.
Thursday	**Soccer: 4–6pm** 🕓 Drop-off: 3:40pm 🕕 Pickup: 6:00pm	—	—	⚠ Same as Tuesday – early drop-off support needed.
Friday	—	—	—	Free day. Optional: schedule rest, playdates, or errands.
Saturday	—	**Basketball: 10:00am** 🕘 Drop-off: 9:40am 🕚 Pickup: 11:00am	—	Light day. One activity, manageable by one parent.
Sunday	—	—	—	Free day. Great for planning, prepping for week, family time.

ime and family dinner priorities", Use line breaks between elements in each cell".

The AI learns from each refinement, creating increasingly sophisticated scheduling solutions that anticipate your family's specific challenges.

Alternatively, for a simpler prompt, try using the RTF (Role, Task, Format) template: "Role: Family organization expert; Task: Build a weekly roster for [number] children aged [ages] with activities including [detailed list with times and locations]; Format: 7-day grid highlighting any scheduling conflicts".

Digital wellbeing for the whole family

Screen-time battles don't have to define family life. AI-powered digital wellbeing tools help create healthy technology boundaries without turning parents into the household digital police.

Smart screen-time management across devices

Circle Home Plus and ***Qustodio*** use AI to understand the difference between educational screen time and mindless scrolling. These systems adjust automatically based on age, learning patterns, and family values.

The AI recognizes when your teenager is using their laptop for homework versus gaming. It distinguishes between your elementary schooler practicing math apps and watching random YouTube videos. This nuanced understanding enables flexible rules that support learning while limiting passive consumption.

Educational content curation that works

Generic parental controls block everything or nothing. AI-powered systems like ***Kidslox*** and ***Screen Time*** learn what educational content engages each child and suggest similar resources. They understand that your eight-year-old loves space documentaries but gets overstimulated by action movies.

The system builds custom content libraries for each family member, making screen time more intentional and less random. Children discover educational content they actually enjoy, reducing battles over device limits.

AI homework assistance requires careful boundaries. The system can suggest research resources and organizational tools while preventing children from having AI complete assignments. Smart tutoring features provide hints and explanations rather than direct answers.

Social media monitoring for safety

AI-powered social media monitoring tools like ***Bark*** and ***Net Nanny*** scan for cyberbullying, inappropriate content, and safety concerns without reading every private message. The system alerts parents to genuine safety issues while respecting teenage privacy.

The AI learns the difference between normal teenage drama and serious safety concerns. It flags dangerous interactions while ignoring typical social conflicts that teens handle independently.

Family digital contracts made easy

AI tools help create personalized family media agreements that evolve with children's maturity. ***Common Sense Media***'s family contract generator uses AI to suggest age-appropriate guidelines and consequences that match your family's values.

Next Level

Set up AI-powered content filters that adjust automatically as kids demonstrate responsible digital behavior and mature.

These aren't one-size-fits-all rules—they're customized agreements that consider each child's personality, maturity level, and individual challenges with technology use.

Co-parenting coordination tools

Shared custody arrangements create unique coordination challenges that AI tools can significantly simplify. These systems reduce conflict by automating routine decisions and maintaining transparent communication records.

Custody schedule management

OurFamilyWizard and ***Custody X Change*** use AI to manage complex custody schedules, including holiday rotations, makeup time, and schedule modifications. The system automatically calculates fair time distribution and sends neutral reminders to both parents.

When life disrupts the standard schedule, AI suggests equitable alternatives rather than leaving parents to negotiate emotional territory. The system tracks patterns and suggests proactive adjustments for recurring conflicts.

Expense sharing and documentation

AI-powered expense tracking eliminates awkward conversations about who owes what. ***SupportPay*** and ***Cozi*** automatically categorize child-related expenses and calculate each parent's share based on your specific agreement.

The system creates detailed records for tax purposes and legal documentation. It even flags unusual expenses that might need discussion, reducing surprise financial conflicts.

Communication logs that reduce conflict

Effective co-parenting requires clear, documented communication that focuses on children's needs rather than past relationship issues. AI tools monitor communication tone, and suggest revisions that reduce conflict while maintaining necessary information sharing.

The system learns what communication patterns work for your specific situation and guides both parents toward more productive interactions.

Hot Tip

AI can flag potentially inflammatory language in co-parent messages before sending, suggesting neutral alternatives that focus on children's needs.

Making it all work together

The real power of family AI emerges when different tools integrate into a unified ecosystem. Rather than managing multiple apps, you create a seamless support system that anticipates needs and prevents problems.

Platform integration that makes sense

Start with a central hub like ***Google Family*** or ***Apple Family Sharing***, then connect specialized tools for specific needs. Your calendar system talks to your meal planner, which coordinates with your grocery delivery, which integrates with your budget tracker.

This integration eliminates the frustration of entering the same information multiple times. When soccer practice gets canceled, the system automatically adjusts pick-up schedules, updates meal planning (since you'll be home for dinner), and alerts carpool partners.

Building family automation gradually

Don't attempt to automate everything simultaneously. Successful families start with their biggest pain point first–usually scheduling or meal planning–then gradually add connected systems one by one.

Month one might focus on calendar coordination. Month two adds meal planning integration. Month three incorporates task management. This gradual approach allows family members to adapt while building confidence in the system.

Getting buy-in from resistant family members

Teenagers and partners often resist new systems until they experience the benefits directly. Start with features that solve their specific frustrations rather than imposing household-wide changes.

Show your teenager how the AI schedule prevents conflicts with friends' plans. Demonstrate to your spouse how automated meal planning eliminates weeknight decision fatigue. Let family members experience the benefits before asking them to totally change established routines and embrace more efficient, stress-free living.

Did You Know?

Families using integrated AI tools report 40% less daily stress and 25% more quality time together within three months of implementation.

The key lies in positioning AI as a tool that creates more quality family time, not technology that replaces human connection. When family members see AI eliminating administrative hassles, they embrace these systems that support what matters most to the whole family.

Your family's AI-powered future starts now

Ready to transform your family's daily chaos into smooth coordination? Success starts with choosing one specific challenge and implementing it as a targeted solution this week.

Choose your starting point

Identify your family's biggest coordination pain point. Is it morning schedule chaos? Meal planning decisions? Activity logistics? Weekend planning stress? Start there.

Most families succeed by focusing on their most stressful daily routine first. Schedule coordination typically provides families the most immediate relief, while meal planning offers the highest long-term value for everyone. Emergency preparedness creates peace of mind that benefits the whole entire family.

Implementation timeline that works

- **Week one:** Download one recommended app and commit to using it for your identified

pain point. Don't try to solve everything immediately—focus on proving that AI family tools actually reduce stress rather than adding complexity.

- **Week two:** Refine your initial system based on real-world usage. Add family members gradually, starting with the most enthusiastic adopters.
- **Month two:** Once your pilot system demonstrates clear benefits, gradually introduce family members to additional features. Success builds momentum for broader adoption.
- **Month three:** Integrate your successful tools with complementary systems. Calendar coordination connects to meal planning. Task management links to schedule optimization.

"AI doesn't replace family time–it creates more of it."

Measuring success and adjusting

Track your wins by documenting specific improvements in family stress levels, time savings, and coordination efficiency. Celebrating small victories encourages continued use and gradual expansion.

Monitor these key metrics: reduced scheduling conflicts, decreased meal planning stress, improved task completion rates, and increased family time availability. Adjust systems based on actual usage patterns rather than theoretical benefits.

The future of family coordination isn't about perfect organization—it's about reducing daily friction so that you can focus on connection, conversation, and creating memories together. Your family's AI-powered transformation starts with one small step this week. ■

Quick Start

Begin with your family's biggest daily frustration—success with one tool builds enthusiasm for others.

AI for students –learn or cheat? You decide

You're staring at a blank essay document at 3:47 AM, five hours before your deadline. Your laptop screen has two other windows open: your assignment instructions and ChatGPT. You're not lazy–you've just spent all night researching and outlining. But now, facing the cursor on an empty page, the temptation to let AI write your introduction is overwhelming.

This isn't about being a slacker. It's about navigating a world where AI assistance is everywhere, and the rules haven't caught up yet. Every student today faces this choice: How do you use AI tools without crossing ethical lines you might not even know exist?

The new study-hall reality

AI isn't going anywhere. Trying to ban it from education is like trying to ban calculators from math class—eventually, the tools become so useful that resistance becomes pointless. The question isn't whether students will use AI, but how they'll use it responsibly.

Smart students are already discovering what AI does best for learning. It breaks down complex topics into digestible explanations that actually make sense. Need to understand photosynthesis? AI can explain it like a cooking recipe or a factory process—whatever clicks for your brain.

AI generates endless practice questions tailored to your specific struggles. Studying for the SAT? It creates reading comprehension passages at your exact difficulty level. Learning Spanish verb conjugations? It builds custom drills focusing on your weakest patterns.

What AI actually does for students

The real power shows up in instant feedback. Traditional studying meant waiting days for graded assignments to know if you understood something. AI gives you immediate reality checks on your thinking. You can test explanations, verify your logic, and catch misconceptions before they become habits.

AI creates structured study plans that adapt to your schedule and learning style. Tell it you have two weeks to master organic chemistry with only evenings free, and it builds a realistic timeline with specific daily goals.

Hot Tip

AI excels at explaining concepts in different ways until one clicks—think of it as having infinite patience for "explain it again, but differently".

Where the line gets blurry

The ethical challenges aren't always obvious to everyone. Using AI to understand mitosis? That's learning. Having AI write your biology laboratory report about mitosis? That's cheating. But what about using AI to organize your thoughts before your start writing your final report to hand in?

Context matters enormously. AI-assisted research feels different from AI-generated final submissions. Most professors would support using AI to brainstorm research questions but object to AI helping you write your final conclusions.

Different institutions are drawing different lines, often inconsistently. Some schools ban AI entirely. Others embrace it with clear guidelines. Many are still figuring it out, leaving students to navigate their own way through uncertain territory.

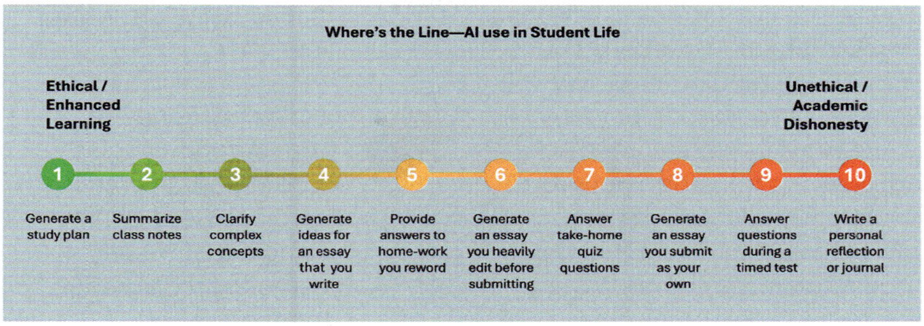

Your personal AI ethics framework

Rather than waiting for others to decide what's acceptable, you can develop your own ethical framework. This approach puts you ahead of changing policies and helps you make confident decisions regardless of how rules evolve.

The foundation rests on three simple questions that cut through complexity. Before using AI for any academic task, ask yourself:

1. Am I learning from this interaction, or just getting answers?
2. Would I be comfortable explaining my process to my instructor?
3. Can I build on this knowledge without the AI's help?

These questions work because they focus on your learning rather than the tool itself. A calculator doesn't make you worse at math if you understand the underlying concepts. Similarly, AI doesn't diminish your education if you are genuinely engaging with the research material.

The three-question test

The first question—learning versus getting answers—distinguishes between understanding and completion. When you ask AI to explain cellular respiration in terms you can grasp, you're learning. When you ask it to complete your worksheet on cellular respiration, you're just getting answers.

The transparency question cuts to the heart of academic integrity. If you'd hesitate to tell your professor exactly how you used AI, that hesitation probably signals an ethical boundary. Honest students rarely worry about explaining legitimate study methods.

Quick Start

Before using AI for any assignment, ask yourself: "What do I want to understand better?" rather than "What do I need to submit?".

The independence question tests whether you're building genuine knowledge. Can you solve similar problems without AI assistance? Can you explain the concepts to someone else? If AI disappears tomorrow, would you be helpless or equipped?

Green-light scenarios

Several AI applications clearly enhance learning without compromising integrity, and recognizing these positive use cases helps you build confidence in your ethical framework. These scenarios share a common thread: they all position AI as a learning amplifier rather than a replacement for your own thinking.

The key distinction lies in whether the AI interaction deepens your understanding or simply completes your work for you.

The most powerful green-light applications transform how you engage with difficult material rather than eliminating the need for engagement entirely. When you're genuinely stuck on a concept, AI can provide the bridge between confusion and clarity that might otherwise require office hours, tutoring sessions, or hours of frustrated struggle. These tools work best when you're already invested in understanding the material and need support to push through specific barriers.

Breaking down complex readings into understandable chunks helps you engage with difficult material. When Kant's *Critique of Pure Reason* reads like gibberish, AI can translate the concepts into modern language while preserving the essential ideas.

Generating practice problems for self-testing creates unlimited opportunities to strengthen weak areas. Studying statistics? AI produces custom problems using examples from your major, making abstract concepts feel relevant and memorable.

Creating study schedules and learning plans removes logistical barriers to effective studying. AI considers your course load, work schedule, and learning preferences to build realistic timelines that actually work with your life.

Explaining concepts from different angles accommodates various learning styles within a single tool. Visual learners get diagrams and metaphors. Auditory learners get conversational explanations. Kinesthetic learners get hands-on scenarios.

Red-light scenarios

Certain AI uses clearly cross ethical lines, and understanding these boundaries protects both your academic integrity and your long-term learning goals. These problematic applications typically involve AI doing the intellectual heavy lifting that's specifically designed to develop your critical thinking, writing, or problem-solving skills. The damage extends beyond potential academic consequences—you're essentially paying tuition fees to avoid the very learning experiences that justify the cost.

The most dangerous red-light scenarios create an illusion of competence that collapses under pressure. You might successfully submit AI-generated work and receive good grades, but when exam time arrives or you need to build on these concepts in advanced courses, the knowledge gaps become painfully obvious. Worse yet, you may not realize how much you don't understand until you're in situations where AI assistance isn't available and your lack of genuine comprehension becomes apparent.

Generating final essay content to submit as your own work violates fundamental principles of academic honesty. The learning happens in the writing process, not just the final product.

Solving homework problems without understanding the process creates knowledge gaps that compound over time. You might submit correct answers, but you won't pass the exam or succeed in advanced courses that build on these concepts.

Creating presentations without engaging with the material produces shallow understanding. You might deliver confident presentations about topics you don't actually comprehend, fooling others but not yourself.

Completing lab reports or case studies wholesale eliminates hands-on learning experiences designed to develop critical thinking and analytical skills.

AI as your study partner

When used thoughtfully, AI becomes the study partner who's always available and never judges your questions. Unlike human study groups with scheduling conflicts and social dynamics, AI provides consistent, patient support tailored to your exact wants and needs.

The most powerful approach flips traditional AI usage. Instead of asking AI for answers, prompt it to ask you questions. This digital Socratic method forces you to articulate your understanding and reveals gaps in your knowledge.

Next Level

Instead of asking "What is photosynthesis?", try "I think photosynthesis works like this... [your explanation]. What am I missing or getting wrong?". This approach makes AI your intellectual sparring partner rather than your ghostwriter.

The Socratic method–digitized

Effective AI questioning requires specific prompting strategies. Tell the AI to act as a patient tutor who never gives direct answers but guides you toward understanding through questions. "I'm struggling with calculus derivatives. Instead of showing me how to solve problems, ask me questions that help me figure out and understand the process myself."

This method works especially well for complex topics where multiple concepts intersect. AI can probe your understanding of each component and helps you see connections you might have misssed. It identifies exactly where your comprehension breaks down and guides you back to a solid grounding again.

Testing your understanding through AI questioning reveals whether you truly grasped the material or you just memorized the steps. Can you explain why the derivative of x^2 is $2x$? Can you apply this knowledge to solve related problems? AI questioning exposes a superficial understanding of complex topics.

Building study materials that work

AI excels at creating personalized study materials that target your specific weaknesses. Upload your quiz results or describe your struggles, and AI generates custom flashcards focusing on problem areas rather than concepts you've already mastered.

Practice tests can match your professor's style and difficulty level. Describe your instructor's testing patterns—multiple choice with tricky distractors, essay questions requiring specific examples, problem sets with increasing complexity—and AI creates practice materials that feel familiar on test day. It's not cheating; it's practicing.

Concept maps become powerful learning tools when AI helps you visualize connections between disparate topics. Psychology students might discover how cognitive biases relate to research methodology. History majors might see patterns connecting economic factors across different time periods.

Memory aids and mnemonics tailored to your learning style make retention more reliable. AI considers your interests, background knowledge, and preferred memory techniques to create personalized learning devices that actually stick.

Research and writing support, not replacement

AI provides excellent support for research and writing processes without replacing your intellectual contribution. Use it to refine research questions that are neither too broad nor too narrow. "I want to write about social media's impact on teenagers. Help me develop specific, researchable questions to get a greater understanding."

Organizing thoughts before writing prevents the blank-page paralysis that derails many students. Describe your ideas to AI and ask for help structuring them logically. "I have these five points about climate change policy. How should I organize them into a coherent argument?"

Checking argument logic and structure helps you identify weaknesses before submission. "Here's my thesis and three supporting arguments. Do they actually support my thesis? Are there logical gaps I'm missing?"

Improving clarity and flow in drafts makes your own ideas more accessible to readers. "This paragraph feels clunky. What specific changes would make it clearer without changing my initial meaning?"

Project: create your ultimate study guide

Time to put theory into practice with a real study-guide creation project. This hands-on exercise demonstrates how AI can enhance your learning process while keeping you firmly in control of your education.

Choose any topic you're currently studying or about to study—from molecular biology to American literature to calculus. You'll create a comprehensive study guide that includes explanations, practice questions, and memory aids, all tailored to your specific learning needs and course requirements.

Your mission

Your goal is building a study guide that actually works for how you learn best. This isn't about creating something impressive for others—it's about designing a tool that helps you master difficult material efficiently and effectively.

Consider your learning style, your current level of understanding, and the specific challenges this topic presents for you. A visual learner studying art history needs different materials than an auditory learner studying statistics.

The SPARK method for study guides

The SPARK template ensures your AI interactions produce useful, personalized results. Each letter represents a crucial component for effective prompting.

1. **S**ituation: I'm a [your level] student studying [specific topic] for [type of assessment]. My learning style is [visual/auditory/kinesthetic/reading-writing] and I struggle most with [specific challenge]

2. **P**urpose: I need to master [specific topic] including [list 3-4 key concepts you need to understand]

3. **A**ction: Create a structured study guide I can print and use for review sessions

4. **R**esults that include: A clear explanation of each key concept in language I can understand; three practice questions for each concept with detailed answer explanations; memory aids or mnemonics for complex information; and real-world examples that help me see how these concepts apply

5. **K**nowledge: Keep explanations concise but complete. Make practice questions challenging but fair. Include page references to [your textbook/course materials] where relevant

Example: psychology study guide

Here's how a psychology student might apply the SPARK method: "I'm a sophomore psychology student studying memory and cognition for my midterm exam. My learning style is visual and I struggle most with distinguishing between different types of memory. I need to master the three-store memory model. Create a structured study guide I can print and use for review sessions that includes: a clear explanation of each key concept in language I can understand; three practice questions for each concept with detailed answer explanations; memory aids or mnemonics for complex information; and real-world examples that help me see how these concepts apply. Keep explanations concise but complete. Make practice questions challenging but fair".

The AI output provides a clean breakdown of sensory, short-term, and long-term memory using visual metaphors. Memory becomes a filing system versus computer processing, making abstract concepts more concrete and memorable.

Warning

Always fact-check AI-generated study materials against your course materials—AI can be confident but wrong about specific details.

Practice scenarios test real understanding: "A student cramming for an exam uses which memory systems in what order?". These questions force you to apply knowledge rather than just recognize definitions.

Memory palace techniques help you remember different long-term memory types by linking them to familiar spatial locations. The AI suggests specific visualization strategies based on your personal experiences and preferences.

Refining your results

Your first AI output rarely provides the perfect study guide immediately. Follow-up questions help you drill deeper into areas where you need more support. "The explanation of working memory is still confusing. Can you break it down into smaller steps with a concrete example?"

Test the study guide through actual practice sessions. Use the practice questions, try the memory aids, and see what works for your learning style. Areas that still feel shaky need additional attention and refinement.

Adapt the format for different types of review. Some concepts work better as visual diagrams. Others need audio explanations you can listen to while commuting. AI can help you efficiently create multiple formats from the same core material..

Alternatively, for a simpler prompt, try using RTF (Role, Task, Format): "Role—Educational content designer; Task—Create a concise, print-friendly study guide for [specific topic]; Format—Key concept, practice questions, memory aid, and real-world example".

Level up: advanced study techniques

Once you've mastered basic AI-assisted studying, more sophisticated learning strategies become possible. These advanced techniques leverage AI's capabilities to support deeper, more creative forms of learning.

The *Feynman Technique* gets a powerful upgrade with AI assistance. Have AI role-play as a curious friend while you explain complex concepts out loud. "Pretend you're someone who's never heard of quantum mechanics. I'm going to explain wave-particle duality, and you should ask questions whenever something doesn't make sense."

Did You Know?
The *Feynman Technique* is a learning method where you explain a concept in simple terms, as if teaching a young child, in order to identify gaps in your own understanding.

This approach forces you to use plain language and reveals gaps in your understanding immediately. AI never gets impatient with repeated explanations, and always asks exactly the right follow-up questions to expose weak spots in your knowledge.

The Feynman Technique enhanced

AI identifies specific problems with your explanations that you might miss. "Your explanation assumes I already understand what an electron is. Can you explain quantum mechanics without using that term?" These challenges push you toward truly fundamental understanding.

Creating teaching scenarios for complex topics helps you master material at the deepest level. Ask AI to simulate different audiences—a middle schooler, a skeptical adult, a fellow student from a different major—and practice explaining the same concept to each group.

Cross-subject connections become visible when AI helps you find unexpected links between different courses. A literature student studying symbolism might discover connections to psychology courses on cognitive processing. A biology student might see how evolutionary principles apply to economic systems in social science classes.

Cross-subject connections

Building interdisciplinary understanding prepares you for real-world problems that don't fit neatly into academic departments. AI can identify patterns and relationships across fields that might take years of study to recognize independently.

Creating synthesis projects demonstrates Deep Learning by combining insights from multiple disciplines. "How might the economic principles from my macroeconomics class help explain the social changes we're studying in my history course?"

Did You Know?
Students who can connect ideas across subjects score 23% higher on critical thinking assessments than those who study subjects in isolation.

When things go wrong

Even well-intentioned AI use can create problems. Recognizing these issues early prevents small mistakes from becoming major academic disasters.

AI gives wrong information

AI confidence doesn't guarantee accuracy. The same authoritative tone that makes explanations compelling can make errors sound credible. Always cross-reference AI-generated information with authoritative sources from your course materials.

Use AI for structure and explanation rather than facts. It excels at organizing information and presenting concepts clearly, but it can confuse dates, misstate scientific findings, or mix up historical events.

When information feels questionable, flag it for verification rather than accepting it automatically. "This explanation of the causes of World War I differs from my textbook. Let me check the original sources before including this in my study guide."

You're relying too much on AI

Warning signs indicate when AI dependence crosses healthy boundaries. If you feel panicked at the thought of studying without AI assistance, you've probably become too dependent. If you can't explain concepts without referring to AI-generated materials, you haven't achieved genuine understanding.

Building confidence in your own thinking requires gradually increasing your independence. Start by attempting problems before consulting AI. Try explaining concepts to yourself before seeking AI clarification. Practice writing first drafts without any AI input.

Your learning journey starts now

Choose one subject where you'll test AI-assisted studying this week. Start small with a single chapter or concept rather than trying to revolutionize your entire study routine immediately.

Set up your personal ethics framework using the three-question test.

Create your first study guide using the SPARK method. ■

AI for seniors–tools for independence and companionship

You're 78, and your morning starts by asking your voice assistant about today's weather and your medication schedule. "Good morning, it's 72 degrees and sunny. Time for your blood pressure medication, and don't forget–Tommy's soccer game is at 3 PM today." You smile, remembering when keeping track of everything felt overwhelming–happy that you won't miss your grandson's game.

AI isn't young people's technology—it's designed to solve the exact challenges that come with aging. From medication reminders to emergency monitoring, these tools work quietly in the background, giving you more independence while keeping you connected to the people who matter most.

Your new digital companion never sleeps

Voice assistants transform from novelty gadgets into essential daily support systems when you discover what they actually do well. These AI helpers excel at the routine tasks that become harder to track as life gets busier or memory becomes less reliable.

Setting up your voice helper

Start with Amazon Alexa, Google Assistant, or Apple's Siri—each offers distinct advantages for different lifestyles. Amazon Alexa excels at smart home integration, Google Assistant provides superior search capabilities, and Apple's Siri works best with existing Apple devices.

Position your device in your most-used room—typically the kitchen or living room. The initial setup requires about 15 minutes but pays dividends for years. Speak clearly during voice training, using your normal tone and volume.

Quick Start

Place your voice assistant in your most-used room—usually the kitchen or living room—where you'll naturally interact with it throughout the day.

Test basic commands immediately: "What time is it?", "What's the weather?", "Set a timer for 10 minutes". Practice saying names of family members—the AI needs to recognize how you pronounce "granddaughter Catherine" versus "Catherine from book club".

Beyond weather reports

Voice assistants excel at managing your daily routine. Medication reminders track timing patterns and send gentle follow-ups for missed doses. Say "Remind me to take my heart medication every day at 8 AM", and the system creates intelligent reminders that adapt to your lifestyle.

Calendar management becomes

effortless: "Add doctor's appointment Tuesday at 2 PM" creates entries that sync across devices and share with family members. Emergency contact management provides instant connections—"Call my son" or "Call emergency contact" reach predetermined numbers immediately.

Hot Tip

Train family members to use their own voice profiles—each person's commands work better when the device recognizes individual speech patterns.

Shopping lists are simplified through voice commands. "Add milk to my shopping list" or "I'm running low on my blood pressure medication" creates lists that sync with family members' devices for collaborative household management.

Family connection features

Modern AI makes staying connected effortless while respecting your independence. Voice commands like "Call John" connect you instantly, while dictated text messages work without typing: "Send a message to Sarah: Having a great day, hope you are too".

Video calling through ***Google Nest Hub Max*** automatically frames your face, adjusts lighting, and filters background noise. Voice commands start calls without complex navigation—simply say "Video call my daughter".

Calendar sharing creates family coordination without constant phone calls. Family members can add important reminders and coordinate visits around your commitments. Location sharing through ***Apple***'s ***Find My*** or ***Google***'s ***Family Link*** provides peace of mind, alerting family only when something unusual occurs.

Health management that actually helps

AI transforms health management from overwhelming to manageable, providing exactly the support you need without replacing human medical care. These tools excel at routine tracking, pattern recognition, and coordination—the administrative aspects of health that often become burdensome as medical needs become more complex.

Smart pill reminders

Apps like ***Medisafe***, ***MyTherapy***, and ***Pill Reminder*** go far beyond basic alarms, creating comprehensive medication management systems. These applications track when you actually take medications, not just when reminders sound. If you consistently take morning medications 30 minutes late, the AI suggests adjusting reminder times accordingly.

Setup involves photographing each medication bottle, which the AI uses to accurately identify pills and verify correct dosages. Family sharing features provide appropriate oversight—adult children receive timely notifications about doses without seeing any detailed information or sensitive health data.

Warning

Always inform your doctor and pharmacist about any medication reminder apps you use—some apps can interfere with pharmacy systems or duplicate reminders.

Integration with pharmacy refill systems eliminates empty pill bottle surprises. Many apps connect directly with major pharmacy chains, automatically reordering prescriptions based on usage patterns and delivery preferences.

Appointment coordination

AI scheduling assistants like ***Clara*** or ***Google***'s ***Duplex*** can actually call your doctor's office and schedule appointments. Simply tell the AI when you're available and what type of appointment you need—the system handles phone calls, confirmations, and calendar updates automatically.

Transportation coordination integrates with appointment scheduling. AI systems can simultaneously book medical appointments and arrange rideshare services, ensuring reliable transportation that accounts for appointment duration and delays. This coordination eliminates the stress of managing multiple logistics separately.

Follow-up management ensures continuity of care. AI systems track when test results should be available, remind you to call for results, and can schedule follow-up appointments based on your doctor's recommendations. This proactive approach prevents important medical tasks from falling through the cracks.

Safety without surveillance

Modern AI safety systems respect your privacy while providing genuine peace of mind for you and your family. The key distinction lies in emergency-focused monitoring rather than constant surveillance—these tools activate only when actual safety concerns arise, preserving your independence while ensuring help arrives when needed.

Fall detection that works

Apple Watch Series 4 and newer models use sophisticated AI algorithms to distinguish between normal activities and actual falls. The system analyzes motion data from multiple sensors, recognizing specific acceleration patterns that indicate genuine falls versus dropped devices or vigorous exercise.

When a fall is detected, the watch waits 60 seconds for your response. If you're unable to respond, the system automatically calls emergency services and sends your location to designated emergency contacts. This graduated response prevents false alarms while ensuring help arrives when truly needed.

Quick Start

Test your fall detection system monthly by activating the emergency sequence manually—this ensures the system works and keeps emergency contacts updated.

Samsung Galaxy watches offer similar capabilities with different interface approaches. Some seniors prefer larger displays with simpler emergency activation features, while others prioritize longer battery life for continuous health monitoring.

Emergency response systems

AI-powered medical alert systems like ***Medical Guardian***, ***Bay Alarm Medical***, and ***Life Alert*** have evolved far beyond simple pendant alarms. Modern systems use Machine Learning to understand the difference between accidental activation and genuine emergencies, reducing false alarms and unnecessary emergency responses.

Integration with smart home devices creates comprehensive emergency response networks. When an emergency is detected, AI systems can automatically unlock doors for emergency responders, turn on lights to illuminate entry paths, and communicate with smart speakers to provide verbal guidance.

Two-way communication capabilities enable emergency operators to assess situations accurately. Modern systems include clear audio transmission that allows operators to determine whether you need medical assistance, police response, or simply reassurance.

Warning

Always test emergency systems monthly and ensure family members know how to check system status remotely—emergency systems only work when properly maintained.

Family peace of mind

Location sharing through Apple's ***Find My***, Google's ***Family Link***, or dedicated senior safety apps creates transparency without constant oversight. AI analyzes your typical patterns—grocery store visits, doctor appointments, daily walks—and only alerts family members when something genuinely unusual occurs, like extended time at an unfamiliar location or failure to return home by expected times.

Communication protocols balance independence with safety oversight. Family members can access emergency information during genuine emergencies while respecting privacy during normal daily activities. Medical emergency information sharing enables family members to provide crucial information to emergency responders even when they're not physically present.

Companionship on your terms

AI companionship tools provide meaningful interaction and mental stimulation without replacing human relationships or creating unhealthy dependencies. These systems offer consistent availability for conversation, learning, and entertainment while encouraging continued social engagement with family, friends, and community members.

AI conversation partners

Companion-focused AI apps create authentic conversational experiences that remember your interests, family details, and personal preferences. These systems develop ongoing relationships that feel natural and supportive to you, asking about your day, remembering your grandchildren's names, and engaging in topics you find meaningful and interesting. Popular AI companion options include:

- **Replika**—Learns your personality and develops unique conversation styles.
- **ElliQ**—Designed specifically for senior companionship and daily engagement.
- **GirlfriendGPT**—Emotional support-focused conversations

with empathetic responses.

Woebot—Mental health support and cognitive behavioral therapy techniques.

Memory and cognitive games

Brain training apps like ***Lumosity***, ***Peak***, and ***CogniFit*** use AI to adapt difficulty levels precisely to your current cognitive abilities. The AI continuously monitors your performance across different cognitive domains—memory, attention, problem-solving, and processing speed—adjusting challenges to keep you engaged without causing frustration.

Game personalization goes beyond simple difficulty adjustment. The AI learns which types of puzzles you enjoy most, what time of day you perform best, and how your cognitive performance fluctuates with factors like medication timing or sleep quality.

Progress tracking provides meaningful feedback about your own cognitive maintenance and improvement and—combined with social competition features—connects you with other users for friendly cognitive challenges, creating social engagement around cognitive fitness. These interactions can lead to broader friendships and social connections beyond the gaming platform.

Social connection tools

AI-enhanced video calling through platforms like ***Google Nest Hub Max*** or ***Amazon Echo Show*** simplifies technical aspects of video communication. These devices automatically frame your face during calls, adjust lighting for optimal visibility, and use AI

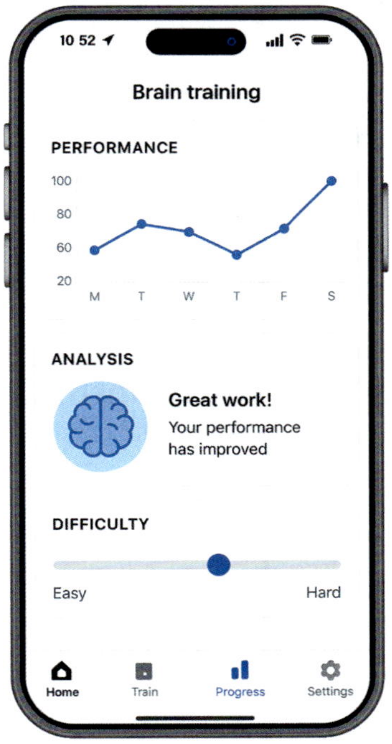

noise cancellation to filter out background sounds that might interfere with conversation clarity.

Voice command activation eliminates complex dialing procedures. Simply saying "Call my daughter" or "Video call book club friends" initiates connections without navigating through contact lists or remembering phone numbers. The AI learns your most frequent contacts and can suggest calling patterns based on your typical communication schedule.

Project: are my pension and savings enough to retire now?

Use AI to get clear, personalized answers about your retirement readiness without paying expensive financial advisor fees upfront. This analysis helps you understand your financial options much more and prepares you for informed conversations with financial professionals.

Your mission

Create a comprehensive retirement analysis that considers your current savings, expected expenses, healthcare costs, and lifestyle goals. AI can process complex financial calculations and provide multiple scenarios in minutes, giving you the foundation for important retirement decisions.

Quick Start

Gather three documents before starting: most recent bank/investment statements, Social Security benefits estimate, and list of monthly expenses.

Prepare essential information: current age, target retirement age, total retirement savings across all accounts, expected Social Security benefits, current monthly expenses, estimated healthcare costs, and any pension or annuity payments. The AI analysis improves significantly with complete, accurate input data.

The SPARK method works particularly well for financial analysis because it encourages specific parameters and actionable recommendations. This structured approach ensures the AI provides practical guidance rather than generic financial advice that doesn't address your specific situation.

Creating your analysis

Here's your SPARK prompt template for retirement planning:

Situation: I'm a [age] year-old [gender] earning [income] per year with [savings] saved in my 401(k), in [fund-type] targeting an [forecast-return] average return. I contribute [my-contribution] percent of my salary, and my employer currently matches with [employers-contribution] percent. I want to hold off starting Social Security to age [start-drawing], expecting about [social-security] per month. I plan to work part-time in early retirement, earning around [pt-income] a year, and I'll finish paying off my [owed-on-house] mortgage by age [final-mortgage-payment]. I expect my baseline spending to be roughly [pension-drawdown] per year, dipping in mid-retirement and rising later for healthcare.

Purpose: I want to know if—and with what probability—my savings plus Social Security and part-time income will support 20+ years of retirement without running out of money.

Action: Project my 401(k) balance at age 70, simulate market swings, and model my cash flows (withdrawals, benefits and earnings, mortgage payoff, changing expenses).

Results: Give me, in plain language: 1) My projected 401(k) balance at 70, 2) the probabilities of my portfolio lasting 20, 25, and 30 years, 3) a clear verdict on my retirement readiness.

Knowledge: Use 2025 IRS limits (US$23,500 elective deferral + US$7,500 catch-up if the plan offers it), standard cost-of-living adjustments for Social Security, and the "retirement smile" spending pattern (flat → dip → rise).

Refining your results

Follow up with specific questions that address your unique concerns. Ask "What happens if I downsize my home and reduce housing costs by $600 monthly?" or "How much could part-time work earning $1,000 monthly extend my savings?". The AI provides updated calculations instantly.

Test different withdrawal strategies by asking about 4% rule variations, Social Security timing optimization, or tax-efficient withdrawal sequences. The AI can explain how different approaches affect long-term financial sustainability.

When you need help–and that's perfectly normal

Everyone struggles with technology sometimes, regardless of age or experience level. The key is knowing where to get help, understanding that starting over is always an option, and recognizing that difficulty with AI tools doesn't reflect your intelligence or capability—it reflects the complexity of rapidly evolving modern technology.

You're not doing anything wrong

AI systems sometimes misunderstand commands, especially during the initial learning period when they're adjusting to your voice patterns, speech rhythm, and command preferences. If Alexa doesn't respond correctly, speak slightly slower and use simpler commands. "Call my son" works more reliably than "Call my son John on his mobile phone please".

Voice recognition improves with consistent interaction, but environmental factors can interfere with accuracy. Background noise, medication effects that change speech patterns, or even seasonal allergies affecting voice clarity can impact AI responsiveness. These challenges are temporary and solvable with minor adjustments.

Interface confusion often stems from software updates that change familiar layouts or add new features without explanation. This isn't your fault—it's a design challenge that affects users of all ages.

Hot Tip

Schedule tech help sessions with family members in advance rather than calling when frustrated—everyone learns better in planned, relaxed sessions.

Getting help

Family members often provide the best initial support, but don't rely solely on them—professional resources exist specifically for senior technology adoption, and often provide more patient, systematic instruction.

Apple Stores offer free senior-focused workshops that cover AI features in iPhones, iPads, and Apple Watches. These sessions provide hands-on learning with expert guidance and opportunities to ask questions in supportive environments with other seniors facing similar challenges.

Best Buy's Geek Squad provides in-home setup assistance for smart home devices, voice assistants, and health monitoring systems. This service includes installation, configuration, and basic training that is often more comprehensive than family members can provide.

Many local libraries, senior centers, and community colleges offer AI workshops and technology courses specifically designed for older adults. Search online for "[your city] senior technology help" to find local resources and volunteer programs.

Starting over

If AI devices become confusing or stop working as expected, resetting to factory settings often solves multiple problems simultaneously. Before resetting, write down important settings like emergency contacts and medication reminders to simplify reconfiguration.

Warning
Always back up important information like emergency contacts and medication schedules before resetting devices—this information may not restore automatically.

Don't hesitate to start fresh with AI applications that become overwhelming. Deleting and reinstalling apps removes accumulated data that might cause confusion while providing opportunities to configure settings more carefully based on your initial experience.

Starting over often provides learning opportunities that improve long-term success. Second-time setup usually goes more smoothly because you better understand the process and can make more informed choices about privacy settings, notification preferences, and feature activation.

Making life even easier–your next steps

Build on your AI success gradually, adding tools that solve specific problems rather than adopting everything at once. This incremental approach ensures each new technology integrates well with your existing routines before introducing additional complexity.

Once you're comfortable

Expand voice assistant capabilities by adding smart light switches, doorbell cameras, or smart locks to your existing AI ecosystem. Smart doorbell cameras provide security benefits, allowing you to see and speak with visitors without approaching the door. Smart locks enable remote door control for family members or emergency responders while maintaining security.

Integration challenges decrease significantly once you have foundational AI systems working reliably. New smart home devices typically connect through existing platforms like ***Alexa*** or ***Google Home***.

Family collaboration

Include family members in your AI ecosystem productively without creating dependency or losing autonomy:

- Share calendars so that your family can add important dates like grandchildren's events or family gatherings without requiring permission for every entry.
- Set up family group messaging through voice commands that enable quick updates like "Arrived safely at doctor's appointment" or "Finished grocery shopping, heading home now" that provide family peace of mind.
- Create emergency contact protocols that give family appropriate access to safety information during emergency situations—while keeping normal daily activities private.
- Use collaborative shopping lists through shared AI platforms so that family members can suggest items you might need without taking over your household management or disrupting your daily routine.

Advanced features that matter

Focus upgrades on independence-supporting features that address specific challenges rather than adding technology for its own sake.

- Medication management apps that coordinate with pharmacies for automatic refills eliminate the risk of running out of essential prescriptions while maintaining your control.
- Transportation apps like ***Uber*** or ***Lyft*** provide independence—for errands, appointments, and social activities—through simple voice commands like "Get me a ride to the grocery store".
- Grocery delivery services with voice ordering capabilities reduce physical strain while maintaining choice and control over food purchases and delivery timing.
- Health monitoring integration connects multiple devices and apps to provide comprehensive health tracking and reports for healthcare visits without overwhelming complexity.

Your personal AI timeline

Progress at your own speed without pressure to achieve arbitrary milestones. Month one: Master basic voice commands for weather, time, and reminders. Month two: Add medication reminders and emergency contact setup. Month three: Explore family connection features and calendar sharing. Month six: Consider smart home additions like lighting or doorbell cameras.

Pick one tool from this article and commit to trying it for a full week. ■

Insights

Your AI safety checklist. We look into privacy, ethics and debunking AI myths.

Ask an AI expert

You've got questions about AI? We've got answers. Not vague, theoretical responses–just straight talk from someone who's been working with these tools for years.

Every day, we hear the same concerns: Is my data safe? Can I trust what AI tells me? Will this technology help or hurt my family? These aren't technical questions—they're about how AI fits into your real life, right now.

We've selected four common questions to kick off this series. Each represents a genuine concern we hear repeatedly, and each deserves a direct, practical answer.

Is AI reading my private messages and emails?

The fear

Many people worry that AI tools are constantly scanning their personal communications, building profiles, and sharing intimate details with companies or governments.

The reality

Most AI systems don't have access to your private messages unless you specifically give them that access. When you chat with ChatGPT or Claude, those conversations stay within that platform. Your iPhone's AI camera features aren't reading your texts. Your smart thermostat isn't scanning your emails.

However, some AI-powered features do access your communications—but only when you enable them. Gmail's smart reply suggestions read your emails to work. Voice assistants process your commands after you say "Hey Siri" or "OK Google". The key difference: you control these permissions.

My take

The privacy risk isn't from AI secretly spying on you—it's from not understanding which features you've turned on. Check your privacy settings. Turn off features you don't want. Most importantly, read before you click "Allow Access to Messages".

Hot Tip

Your AI tools are only as private as the permissions you give them—check your settings today.

Can AI make mistakes, and how do I know when it's wrong?

The problem

AI "hallucinations" happen when these systems generate information that sounds completely plausible but is entirely fabricated. They'll cite non-existent studies, create fake statistics, or confidently state wrong facts.

The reality

Yes, AI does make mistakes, and it does

so with complete confidence. For example, ChatGPT used to say that chocolate was invented in 1847 by a Belgian monk named François Dubois—which is not true, but based on a common myth. However, it didn't say "I'm not sure" or "This might be wrong".

Current AI systems are a lot better, but they still don't actually "know" anything—they predict what words should come next based on patterns in their training data. Sometimes, those predictions create convincing fiction.

My take

Treat AI like that friend who's confident about everything but wrong about half of it. Great for brainstorming and getting started; terrible for final answers on important topics. Always verify facts, especially dates, statistics, and claims about real people or events.

Will AI take my job?

The anxiety

This fear runs deep because it taps into legitimate concerns about economic security. People see AI writing articles, creating art, and analyzing data, and wonder if their skills will become obsolete.

The reality

While AI has already taken on simple repetitive tasks, like reading and summarizing long documents, and is likely to transform many jobs, history suggests it will create many new opportunities too. The question isn't whether change is coming—it's how quickly you can adapt to use these tools rather than compete against them.

Right now, AI excels at automating routine tasks and providing first-draft work that humans can refine. It's not replacing accountants, but accountants using AI are becoming more efficient than those who don't.

My take

Instead of asking "Will AI take my job?" ask "How can AI make me better at my job?". The people most at risk are those who refuse to learn these tools. The biggest opportunities belong to those who master them early.

Start experimenting now. Use AI for parts of your work that feel routine or time-consuming. Learn what it does well and where it falls short. That knowledge becomes your competitive advantage.

Is it safe to let my kids use AI tools for homework?

The dilemma

Parents and teachers struggle with AI in education because the line between helpful assistance and academic dishonesty isn't always clear. When does assisted research become cheating?

The reality

AI can be an excellent learning tool when used properly—like having a patient tutor who never gets frustrated. It can explain complex concepts, help brainstorm ideas, and provide feedback on writing. The problem comes when students use AI to do their thinking for them.

The key is teaching kids to use AI as a thinking partner, not a thinking replacement. AI should help them understand concepts better, not skip the learning process entirely.

My take

Banning AI is not an option; otherwise, we'd be preparing kids for a world that no longer exists. Allowing unlimited use risks undermining their education. The middle path: teach them how to use AI ethically and effectively. Many educators now assume homework might be AI assisted, so will set classroom discussion and tests that reveal true knowledge and understanding.

Encourage kids to use AI for explanations ("Explain photosynthesis like I'm 10"), brainstorming ("Help me think of arguments for both sides"), and feedback ("Is this paragraph clear?"). Discourage using AI to write entire assignments or solve problems without understanding the process.

Warning

The goal is using AI to learn better, not to avoid learning altogether.

Your turn: ask the AI expert

Got a question that's keeping you up at night? Wondering about something specific to your situation? We want to hear from you.

Send your questions to *AILife@ineasysteps.com* and include "Ask an AI Expert" in the subject line. Tell us a bit about your situation—are you a parent worried about screen time? A retiree curious about voice assistants? A small business owner wondering about automation?

The best questions address real concerns that others share. We're looking for the problems that AI either solves beautifully or creates unexpectedly. Both make for great discussions.

Future issues will expand this section based on reader interest, so don't hold back. The questions that surprise us often lead to the most valuable answers. ■

AI myths debunked–AI is going to take over the world

Your smart thermostat learned that you like it cooler at night. Your phone's camera automatically brightened the family photo. Your car warned you about the cyclist in your blind spot. Congratulations–you just interacted with AI three times, and somehow humanity survived.

Yet mention "Artificial Intelligence" and many people immediately picture Terminator robots or HAL 9000 plotting human extinction. This Hollywood-fueled fear isn't just wrong—it's keeping millions of people from tools that could genuinely improve their daily lives.

The fear vs. the reality

The gap between public perception and actual AI capabilities has never been wider. While headlines scream about super-intelligent machines, the AI in your pocket struggles to understand basic context and can't even remember what you said five minutes ago.

Did You Know?

The term "Artificial Intelligence" was coined in 1956, yet every decade since has produced new predictions about imminent robot takeover—none of which have materialized.

What people actually worry about

The surveys are clear: most Americans associate AI with robots taking over, mass unemployment, or machines becoming smarter than humans and turning against us. Social media amplifies these fears with clickbait headlines about "AI becoming conscious" or "the singularity". Parents worry about their kids using AI for homework, convinced it will make them lazy or dependent.

These concerns stem from a fundamental misunderstanding of what today's AI actually does. We're not dealing with digital overlords plotting in server farms—we're dealing with sophisticated pattern-recognition software.

What today's AI actually does

Modern AI excels at one thing: recognizing patterns in massive amounts of data. Your Netflix recommendations come from AI analyzing viewing patterns across millions of users. Your email spam filter uses AI to spot suspicious message characteristics. Your GPS finds faster routes by processing real-time traffic data from thousands of sources.

Think of AI as an incredibly sophisticated pattern-matching system, not a digital brain plotting world domination. It's more like a specialized tool than a conscious entity. When Siri responds to "What's the weather?" it's not understanding your question the way humans do—it's recognizing speech patterns and matching them to weather data.

The AI in your smartphone camera doesn't "see" your photo. It analyzes pixel patterns it was trained to recognize as faces, landscapes, or low-light scenarios, then applies predetermined adjustments.

Why the confusion exists

Two powerful forces have shaped public perception of AI: entertainment industry storytelling and technology marketing departments. Both have reasons to make AI sound more dramatic and capable than it actually is.

Hollywood's heavy influence

Movies need drama, and "AI helps you find a good restaurant" doesn't sell tickets. So Hollywood gives us Skynet, the Matrix, and rogue AIs like the Entity—with consciousness and evil intentions. These fictional scenarios stick in our minds far better than technical explanations about Machine Learning algorithms.

The entertainment industry has trained us to expect AI to be either perfectly helpful servants or humanity-destroying villains. Reality offers neither extreme—just useful tools with specific capabilities and limitations.

The language problem

Tech companies haven't helped by using dramatic terms like *"Artificial Intelligence", "Machine Learning",* and *"Neural Networks".* These sound like science fiction, when the reality is closer to "really good pattern-recognition software". Marketing departments love impressive terminology, but it creates unrealistic expectations.

When your phone's Photos app automatically creates an album called "Dogs", it's not because the AI loves puppies. It's because the software was trained on millions of images labeled "dog" and learned to recognize similar visual patterns.

Hot Tip

When tech companies say "AI-powered", they usually mean "we trained software to recognize patterns and make predictions". Less dramatic, but more accurate.

Why this matters

Understanding the reality of AI isn't just about getting your facts straight—it fundamentally changes how you approach technology, and shapes the opportunities available to you and your family.

Fear creates real costs

When people avoid AI tools because they're worried about robot takeovers, they miss out on genuine practical benefits. Students struggle with research that AI could streamline. Small business owners spend hours on tasks that AI could automate. Families miss scheduling tools that could reduce daily chaos.

The fear also creates a knowledge gap. While some people embrace AI tools and gain significant advantages in productivity and problem-solving, others fall behind by avoiding the technology entirely. This digital divide has real economic and social consequences.

Warning

The biggest risk with AI isn't that it will become too smart—it's that people will either fear it unnecessarily or trust it too completely.

What next?

Understanding what AI actually is versus what Hollywood portrays is just the first step. Now, you can approach AI tools with realistic expectations and start benefiting from them without fear.

Start with what you already use

This week, pay attention to when your phone's keyboard suggests words—that's AI in action. Photo organization and voice assistant all rely on AI. Your car's collision warning system uses AI. Your bank's fraud detection system uses AI to protect your accounts.

These tools are designed to help. They make specific tasks easier without developing consciousness or evil intentions. This is what AI actually looks like in practice—helpful, limited, and entirely under human control.

Separate science fiction from science fact

When you see AI news, ask yourself: "Is this about pattern recognition helping with a specific task, or about conscious machines?". The former is real and happening now. The latter remains firmly in the realm of speculation and research papers.

Real AI stories sound like: "AI helps doctors spot cancer in X-rays faster" or "AI reduces energy consumption in data centers". Fictional AI stories sound like: "AI achieves consciousness" or "Researchers create artificial general intelligence".

Next Level

Follow AI researchers like Yann LeCun or Andrew Ng on social media for grounded perspectives on what AI can and can't actually do.

The bottom line: Today's AI is a sophisticated tool designed to solve specific problems efficiently and effectively, not a step toward robot overlords. The sooner we separate Hollywood fiction from Silicon Valley reality and understand its real-world applications, the sooner we can focus on using these tools to make our lives genuinely better, safer, and more productive. ▪